Czech
Phrase Book
&
Dictionary

Berlitz Publishing
New York   Munich   Singapore

Contacting the Editors
Every effort has been made to provide accurate information in this publication, but changes are inevitable. The publisher cannot be responsible for any resulting loss, inconvenience or injury. We would appreciate it if readers would call our attention to any errors or outdated information. We also welcome your suggestions; if you come across a relevant expression not in our phrase book, please contact us: Berlitz Publishing, 193 Morris Avenue, Springfield, NJ 07081, USA. Email: comments@berlitzbooks.com

All Rights Reserved
© 2008 Berlitz Publishing/APA Publications GmbH & Co. Verlag KG, Singapore Branch, Singapore

Berlitz Trademark Reg. U.S. Patent Office and other countries. Marca Registrada. Used under license from Berlitz Investment Corporation.

First Printing: May 2008
Printed in Singapore

Publishing Director: Sheryl Olinsky Borg
Senior Editor/Project Manager: Lorraine Sova
Translation: Quendi Language Services
Cover Design: Claudia Petrilli
Interior Design: Derrick Lim, Juergen Bartz
Production Manager: Elizabeth Gaynor
Cover Photo: © Henryk T. Kaiser/age fotostock
Interior Photos: p. 12 © Studio Fourteen/Brand X Pictures/age fotostock; p. 16 © 2007 Jupiterimages Corporation; p. 18 © Pixtal/age fotostock; p. 32-33 © Roman Korchuk, 2006/ Shutterstock, Inc.; p. 39 © Corbis/fotosearch.com; p. 46 © Purestock/Alamy; p. 52 © Quendi Language Services; p. 56 © Stockbyte Photography/2002-07 Veer Incorporated; p. 67 © Quendi Language Services; p. 74 © Javier Larrea/Pixtal/age fotostock; p. 78 © Netfalls/2003-2007 Shutterstock, Inc.; p. 102 © Chris Warham/Alamy; p. 106 © Imageshop.com; p. 111 © image100/Corbis; p. 112 © 2007 Jupiterimages Corporation; p. 115 © Ivo Brezina/2003-2007 Shutterstock, Inc.; p. 118 © 2007 Jupiterimages Corporation; p. 126 © Louis Turner/Alamy; p. 134 © 2007 Jupiterimages Corporation; p. 142 © Jupiterimages/Brand X/Corbis; p. 144 © Stockbyte/Fotosearch.com; p. 148 © Corbis/2006 Jupiterimages Corporation; p. 150 © David McKee/2003-2007 Shutterstock, Inc.; p. 151, 160 © 2007 Jupiterimages Corporation; inside back cover: ©H.W.A.C.

Contents

Survival ───────────────

Food

People

Fun

Special Needs

Resources

Dictionary

Pronunciation

This section is designed to make you familiar with the sounds of Czech using our simplified phonetic transcription. You'll find the pronunciation of the Czech letters and sounds explained below, together with their "imitated" equivalents. To use this system, found throughout the phrase book, simply read the pronunciation as if it were English, noting any special rules below.

Stress in Czech falls on the first syllable of a word, though it is not as pronounced as in English. Prepositions in Czech are generally pronounced together with their object as a single word, so the stress falls on the preposition:

Kolik to stojí na den? <u>koh</u>·lihk toh' <u>stoh</u>·yee <u>nah</u>·dehn
How much is it per day?

Consonants

Letter	Approximate Pronunciation	Symbol	Example	Pronunciation
c	like ts in cats	ts	**cesta**	<u>tsehs</u>·tah
č	like ch in church	ch	**klíč**	kleech
ch	like ch in the Scottish loch	kh	**chyba**	<u>khih</u>·bah
ď	like d + y	dy	**láďa**	<u>lah</u>·dya
g	like g in good	g	**galerie**	<u>gah</u>·leh·rih·yeh
j	like y in yes	y	**jídlo**	<u>yeeh</u>·dloh
ň	like ny in canyon; the apostrophe indicates a softening of the sound	n'	**píseň**	<u>peeh</u>·sehn'

Letter	Approximate Pronunciation	Symbol	Example	Pronunciation
ř	like r + zh, run together	rzh	řepa	<u>rzheh</u>·pah
r	as in English, but rolled	r	ruka	<u>roo</u>·kah
s	like s in seat	s	sobota	<u>soh</u>·boh·tah
š	like sh in short	sh	šest	shehst
ť	like tu in tune; the apostrophe indicates a softening of the sound	t'	chuť	khoot'
v	like v in vest	v	víno	<u>vee</u>·noh
w	found in foreign words only	v	watt	vaht
z	like z in zoo	z	zázemí	<u>zah</u>·zeh·mee
ž	like s in pleasure	zh	žena	<u>zheh</u>·nah

Letters b, d, f, h, k, l, m, n, p, t, v are generally pronounced as in English.

Vowels

Vowels in Czech marked with ´ are long vowels; these should be lengthened when pronounced. The length of the vowel is an essential feature since it can differentiate the meaning of words that are otherwise written with the same spelling. Throughout this book, long vowels in the pronunciation column are marked with bold.

Letter	Approximate Pronunciation	Symbol	Example	Pronunciation
a	like a in father	ah	**tady**	<u>tah</u>·dih
á	like a in father, but longer	ah	**máma**	<u>mah</u>·mah
e	like e in met	eh	**den**	dehn
é	like e in met, but longer	eh	**mléko**	<u>mleh</u>·koh
i/y	like i in bit	ih	**pivo**	<u>pih</u>·voh
í/ý	like ee in see	ee	**bílý**	<u>bee</u>·lee
o	like o in hotel	oh	**slovo**	<u>sloh</u>·voh
ó	like o in hotel, but longer	oh	**gól**	gohl
u	like oo in book	oo	**ruka**	<u>roo</u>·kah
ú/ů	like oo in book, but longer	oo	**úkol, vůz**	<u>oo</u>·kol, voos

Diphthongs

Letter	Approximate Pronunciation	Symbol	Example	Pronunciation
au	like ow in cow	ow	**auto**	<u>ow</u>·toh
ou	like the exclamation oh	oh	**mouka**	<u>moh</u>·kah

Czech is a Slavic language, closely related to Slovak, Russian, Polish and Bulgarian. However, unlike Russian and Bulgarian, Czech uses the Roman alphabet. Many Czech and English words have a common origin in Latin, for example: bratr (brother) and sestra (sister).

Czech is a highly inflected language. This means that word endings change to signal grammatical functions such as gender, number, case, etc.

How to Use This Book

These are the most essential phrases in each section.

Sometimes you see two alternatives in italics, separated by a slash. Choose the one that's right for your situation.

Essential

I'm here on *vacation [holiday]/business.*

Jsem zde *na dovolené/služebně*. yeh·sem zdeh *nah·doh·voh·leh·neh/sloo·zhehb·nyeh*

I'm going to...

Jedu do... Yeh·doo doh...

I'm staying at the...Hotel.

Ubytoval♂/Ubytovala♀ jsem se v hotelu... oo·bih·toh·vahl♂/oo·bih·toh·vah·lah♀ ysehm se fhoh·teh·loo...

You May See...

K NÁSTUPIŠTÍM

to the platforms

INFORMACE

information

REZERVACE

reservations

Train

Where *is/are*...?

Kde *je/jsou*...? gdeh *yeh/ysoh*...

– the ticket office

– **pokladna** poh·klahd·nah

– the information desk

– **informace** ihn·fohr·mah·tseh

– the luggage lockers

– **schránky na zavazadla** shrahn·kih nah zah·vah·zah·dlah

Words you may see are shown in *You May See* boxes.

Any of the words or phrases preceded by dashes can be plugged into the sentence above.

Czech phrases appear in red.

Read the simplified pronunciation as if it were English. For more on pronunciation, see page 7.

Ticketing

Can I buy a ticket on the *bus/train*?

Mohu si koupit jízdenku *v autobusu/ve vlaku*? <u>moh</u>·hoo sih <u>koh</u>·piht <u>yeez</u>·dehn·koo <u>fow</u>·toh·boo·soo/<u>vehvlah</u>·koo

I'd like to...my reservation.

Chtěl♂/Chtěla♀ bych...moji rezervaci. khtyehl♂/<u>khtyeh</u>·lah♀ bihkh...<u>moh</u>·yih <u>reh</u>·zehr·vah·tsih

When different gender forms apply, the masculine form is followed by ♂; feminine by ♀.

– cancel

– **zrušit** <u>zroo</u>·shiht

– change

– **změnit** <u>zmyeh</u>·niht

– confirm

– **potvrdit** <u>pohtfr</u>·dih

▶ For numbers, see page 170.

The arrow indicates a cross reference where you'll find related phrases.

Information boxes contain relevant country, culture and language tips.

i At some banks, cash can be obtained from ATMs with Visa, Eurocard, American Express and many other international cards. Instructions are often given in English. You can also change money at travel agencies and hotels, but the rate will not be as good.

You May Hear...

Jakými aerolinkami letíte? <u>yah</u>·kee·mih <u>ah</u>·eh·roh·lihn·kah·mih <u>leh</u>·tee·teh

What airline are you flying?

Expressions you may hear are shown in *You May Hear* boxes.

Color-coded side bars identify each section of the book.

11

▼ Survival

Arrival and Departure

Essential

I'm here on *vacation* [*holiday*]/*business*.	**Jsem zde *na dovolené/služebně*.** ysehm zdeh *nah·doh·voh·leh·neh/sloo·zhehb·nyeh*
I'm going to...	**Jedu do...** Yeh·doo doh...
I'm staying at the...Hotel.	**Ubytoval♂/Ubytovala♀ jsem se v hotelu...** oo·bih·toh·vahl♂/oo·bih·toh·vah·lah♀ ysehm se fhoh·teh·loo...

You May Hear...

Letenku/Cestovní pas, prosím. leh·tehn·koo/tsehs·tohv·nee pahs proh·seem	Your *ticket/passport*, please.
Jaký je účel vaší cesty? yah·kee yeh oo·chehl vah·shee tseh·stih	What's the purpose of your visit?
Kde jste ubytovaný? gdeh ysteh oo·bih·toh·vah·nee	Where are you staying?
Jak dlouho tady budete? yahk dloh·hoh tah·dih boo·deh·teh	How long are you staying?
S kým tady jste? skeem tah·dih ysteh	Who are you with?

Passport Control and Customs

I'm just passing through.	**Pouze projíždím.** poh·zeh proh·yeezh·deem
I would like to declare...	**Rád♂/Ráda♀ bych přihlásil♂/přihlásila♀ k proclení...** raht♂/rah·dah♀ bihkh przhih·hlah·sihl♂/przhih·hlah·sih·lah♀ kproh·tsleh·nee...
I have nothing to declare.	**Nemám nic k proclení.** neh·mahm nihts kproh·tsleh·nee

You May Hear...

Máte něco k proclení? <u>mah</u>·teh <u>nyeh</u>·tsoh <u>kproh</u>·tsleh·nee

Do you have anything to declare?

Za tohle musíte platit clo. zah <u>toh</u>·leh <u>moo</u>·see·teh <u>plah</u>·tiht tsloh

You must pay duty on this.

Otevřte laskavě tuhle *tašku/kufr*. <u>oh</u>·teh·vrzhteh <u>lahs</u>·kah·vyeh <u>too</u>·hleh <u>tahsh</u>·koo/koofr

Please open this *bag/suitcase*.

You May See...

CELNÍ PROHLÍDKA	customs
ZBOŽÍ CLA PROSTÉ	duty-free goods
ZBOŽÍ K PROCLENÍ	goods to declare
NIC K PROCLENÍ	nothing to declare
PASOVÁ KONTROLA	passport control
POLICIE	police

Money and Banking

Essential

Where's...?

Kde je...? gdeh yeh...

– the ATM

– **bankomat** <u>bahn</u>·koh·maht

– the bank

– **banka** <u>bahn</u>·kah

– the currency exchange office

– **směnárna** <u>smyeh</u>·nahr·nah

What time does the bank *open/close*?

V kolik *otvírají/zavírají* banku? <u>fkoh</u>·lihk <u>oht</u>·fee·rah·yee/<u>zah</u>·vee·rah·yee <u>bahn</u>·koo

I'd like to change dollars/pounds into crowns.	**Chtěl♂/Chtěla♀ bych si vyměnit *dolary/ libry* na koruny.** khtyehl♂/<u>khtyeh</u>·lah♀ bihkh sih <u>vih</u>·myeh·niht <u>*doh*</u>·*lah·rih/libb·rih* <u>nah</u>·koh·roo·nih
I'd like to cash some travelers checks [cheques].	**Chtěl♂/Chtěla♀ bych si vyměnit cestovní šeky.** khtyehl♂/<u>khtyeh</u>·lah♀ bihkh sih <u>vih</u>·myeh·niht <u>tsehs</u>·tohv·nee <u>sheh</u>·kih

ATM, Bank and Currency Exchange

Can I exchange currency here?	**Mohu si tady vyměnit peníze?** <u>moh</u>·hoo sih <u>tah</u>·dih <u>vih</u>·myeh·niht <u>peh</u>·nee·zeh
What's the exchange rate?	**Jaký je kurz?** <u>yah</u>·kee yeh koors
How much is the fee?	**Kolik si účtujete provizi?** <u>koh</u>·lihk sih <u>ooch</u>·too·yeh·teh <u>proh</u>·vih·zih
I've lost my travelers checks [cheques].	**Ztratil♂/Ztratila♀ jsem cestovní šeky.** <u>strah</u>·tihl♂/<u>strah</u>·tih·lah♀ ysehm <u>tsehs</u>·tohv·nee <u>sheh</u>·kih
My card was lost.	**Ztratil♂/Ztratila♀ jsem kartu.** <u>strah</u>·tihl♂/<u>strah</u>·tih·lah♀ ysehm <u>kahr</u>·too
My credit cards have been stolen.	**Ukradli mi kreditní karty.** <u>oo</u>·krahd·lih mih <u>kreh</u>·diht·nee <u>kahr</u>·tih
My card doesn't work.	**Moje karta nefunguje.** <u>moh</u>·yeh <u>kahr</u>·tah <u>neh</u>·foon·goo·yeh

▶ For numbers, see page 170.

You May See...

VLOŽTE KARTU	insert card
STORNO	cancel

OPRAVA	clear
ZADEJTE PIN	enter PIN
BĚŽNÝ ÚČET	from checking [current account]
ZŮSTATEK	from savings
STVRZENKA	receipt

 Banky (banks) are generally open Monday through Friday from 8 a.m. to 5 p.m. with a one-hour lunch break around noon. ATMs are available at most banks, but a commission is charged upon cash withdrawal. **Směnárne** (currency exchange offices) operate in large towns and cities. They are usually open from Monday to Friday from 8 a.m. to 6 p.m. with a one-hour break around noon.

You May See...

The monetary unit is the **Česká koruna**, **Kč** (Czech crown), plural **korun**, which is divided into 100 **haléřů**, **h**.
Coins: 10, 20 and 50 **h**; 1, 2, 5, 10 and 20 **Kč**
Notes: 20, 50, 100, 200, 500, 1000, 2000 and 5000 **Kč**

Transportation

Essential

How do I get to town?	**Jak se odtud dostat do mešta?** yahk seh <u>ohd</u>·tood <u>dohs</u>·taht doh <u>meh</u>·shtah
Where's...?	**Kde je...?** gdeh yeh...
– the airport	– **letiště** <u>leh</u>·tihsh·tyeh
– the train [railway] station	– **nádraží** <u>nah</u>·drah·zhee
– the bus station	– **autobusové nádraží** <u>ow</u>·toh·boo·soh·veh <u>nah</u>·drah·zhee
– the subway [underground] station	– **stanice metra** <u>stah</u>·nih·tseh <u>meht</u>·rah
How far is it?	**Jak je to daleko?** yahk yeh toh <u>dah</u>·leh·koh
Where can I buy tickets?	**Kde si mohu koupit jízdenku?** gdeh sih <u>moh</u>·hoo <u>koh</u>·piht <u>yeez</u>·dehn·koo
A one-way [single] ticket.	**Jedním směrem.** <u>yehd</u>·neem <u>smyeh</u>·rehm
A round-trip [return] ticket.	**Zpáteční.** <u>spah</u>·tehch·nee
How much?	**Kolik?** <u>koh</u>·lihk
Are there any discounts?	**Jsou nějaké slevy?** ysoh <u>nyeh</u>·yah·keh <u>sleh</u>·vih
Which *gate/ platform*?	**Který *východ/nástupiště*?** kteh·ree <u>vee</u>·khohd/<u>nahs</u>·too·pihsh·tyeh
Which line?	**Která linka?** <u>kteh</u>·rah <u>lihn</u>·kah
Where can I get a taxi?	**Kde najdu taxík?** gdeh <u>nahy</u>·doo <u>tah</u>·kseek

Please take me to this address.	**Dovezte mě laskavě na tuhle adresu.** doh·vehs·teh myeh <u>lahs</u>·kah·vyeh nah <u>too</u>·hleh <u>ahd</u>·reh·soo
Where can I rent a car?	**Kde si mohu půjčit auto?** gdeh sih <u>moh</u>·hoo <u>pooy</u>·chiht <u>ow</u>·toh
A map please.	**Prosím mapu.** <u>proh</u>·seem <u>mah</u>·poo

Ticketing

When's...to Prague?	**V kolik je...do Prahy?** <u>fkoh</u>·lihk yeh...doh <u>prah</u>·hih
– the (first) bus	**– (první) autobus** (prvnee) <u>ow</u>·toh·boos
– the (next) flight	**– (další) let** (<u>dahl</u>·shee) leht
– the (last) train	**– (poslední) vlak** (<u>pohs</u>·lehd·nee) vlahk
Where can I buy *train/plane* tickets?	**Kde si mohu koupit *jízdenku/letenku*?** gdeh sih <u>moh</u>·hoo <u>koh</u>·piht *<u>yeez</u>·dehn·koo/ <u>leh</u>·tehn·koo*
For *today/ tomorrow*.	**Na *dnešek/zítřek*.** nah <u>dneh</u>·shehk/ zee·trzhehk

▶ For days, see page 172.

▶ For time, see page 172.

...*plane/train* ticket.	**Letenka/Jízdenka...** leh·tehn·kah/ yeez·dehn·kah...
– A one-way [single]	– **jedním směrem** yehd·neem smyeh·rehm
– A round-trip [return]	– **zpáteční** spah·tehch·nee
– A first class	– **do první** doh·prvnee
– An economy class	– **ekonomické třídy** eh·koh·noh·mihts·keh trzhee·dih
How much?	**Kolik?** koh·lihk
Is there a discount for...?	**Je sleva pro...?** yeh sleh·vah proh...
– children	– **děti** dyeh·tih
– students	– **studenty** stoo·dehn·tih
– senior citizens	– **starší občany** stahr·shee ohp·chah·nih
I have an e-ticket.	**Mám elektronický lístek.** mahm eh·lehk·troh·nihts·kee lees·tehk
Can I buy a ticket on the *bus/train*?	**Mohu si koupit jízdenku *v autobusu/ve vlaku*?** moh·hoo sih koh·piht yeez·dehn·koo *fow·toh·boo·soo/vehvlah·koo*
I'd like to...my reservation.	**Chtěl♂/Chtěla♀ bych...moji rezervaci.** khtyehl♂/khtyeh·lah♀ bihkh...moh·yih reh·zehr·vah·tsih
– cancel	– **zrušit** zroo·shiht
– change	– **změnit** zmyeh·niht
– confirm	– **potvrdit** pohtfr·diht

In Czech, there are different words used for "ticket", depending on how you are traveling. **Letenka** is used for plane ticket and **jízdenka** for train or bus ticket. The generic **lístek** describes all tickets but is rarely used.

Plane

Getting to the Airport

How much is a taxi to the airport?	**Kolik stojí taxík na letiště?** <u>koh</u>·lihk <u>stoh</u>·yee tah·kseek <u>nah</u>·leh·tihsh·tyeh
To...Airport, please.	**Na letiště..., prosím.** <u>nah</u>·leh·tihsh·tyeh <u>proh</u>·seem
My airline is...	**Letím aerolinkami...** <u>leh</u>·teem <u>ah</u>·eh·roh·lihn·kah·mih...
My flight leaves at...	**Moje letadlo odlétá v...** <u>moh</u>·yeh <u>leh</u>·tahd·loh <u>ohd</u>·leh·tah f...

▶ For time, see page 172.

I'm in a rush.	**Mám naspěch.** mahm <u>nahs</u>·pyehkh
Can you take an alternate route?	**Můžete jet jinou cestou?** <u>moo</u>·zheh·teh yeht <u>yih</u>·noh <u>tsehs</u>·toh
Can you drive *faster/slower*?	**Můžete jet *rychleji/pomaleji*?** <u>moo</u>·zheh·teh yeht <u>rih</u>·khleh·yih/<u>poh</u>·mah·leh·yih

You May Hear...

Jakými aerolinkami letíte? <u>yah</u>·kee·mih <u>ah</u>·eh·roh·lihn·kah·mih <u>leh</u>·tee·teh	What airline are you flying?
Vnitrostátní nebo mezinárodní? <u>vnih</u>·troh·staht·nee <u>neh</u>·boh meh·zih·nah·rohd·nee	Domestic or international?
Který terminál? <u>kteh</u>·ree <u>tehr</u>·mih·nahl	What terminal?

You May See...

PŘÍLETY	arrivals
ODLETY	departures
VÝDEJ ZAVAZADEL	baggage claim

VNITROSTÁTNÍ	domestic flights
MEZINÁRODNÍ	international flights
REGISTRACE	check-in desk
KONTROLA LETENEK	ticket check-in
VÝCHODY	departure gates

Check-in and Boarding

Where is the check-in desk for flight...?	**U které přepážky se odbavuje let...?** oo·kteh·reh przheh·pah·zhkih seh ohd·bah·voo·yeh leht...
My name is...	**Jmenuji se...** ymeh·noo·yih seh...
I'm going to...	**Jedu do...** yeh·doo doh...
How much luggage is allowed?	**Kolik zavazadel si můžu vzít?** koh·lihk zah·vah·zah·dehl sih **moo**·zhoo vzeet
Which gate does flight...leave from?	**Z kterého východu linka...odlétá?** skteh·reh·hoh vee·khoh·doo lihn·kah... ohd·leh·tah
I'd like *a window/ an aisle* seat.	**Chtěl♂/Chtěla♀ bych místo u *okna/uličky*.** khtyehl♂/khtyeh·lah♀ bihkh **mees**·toh oo *ohk·nah/oo·lihch·kih*
When do we *leave/ arrive*?	**V kolik to *odlétá/přistává?*** fkoh·lihk toh ohd·leh·tah/przhihs·tah·vah
Is the flight...delayed?	**Let...má zpoždění?** leht...mah spozhzh·dyeh·nee
How late will it be?	**Jaké bude mít zpoždění?** yah·keh boo·deh meet spozhzh·dyeh·nee

You May Hear...

| **Další!** dahl·shee | Next! |
| ***Letenku/Cestovní pas*, prosím.** leh·tehn·koo/ tsehs·tohv·nee pahs proh·seem | Your *ticket/ passport*, please. |

Kolik máte zavazadel? <u>koh</u>·lihk <u>mah</u>·teh <u>zah</u>·vah·zah·dehl	How much luggage do you have?
Máte nadváhu. <u>mah</u>·teh <u>nahd</u>·vah·huh	You have excess luggage.
Tohle je na příruční zavazadlo příliš *těžké/velké.* <u>toh</u>·hleh yeh nah przhee·rooch·nee <u>zah</u>·vah·zahd·loh przhee·lihsh *tyezh·keh/vehl·keh*	That's too *heavy/large* for a carry-on [to carry on board].
Balil jste tato zavazadla sám? <u>bah</u>·lihl ysteh <u>tah</u>·toh <u>zah</u>·vah·zah·dlah sahm	Did you pack these bags yourself?
Dal vám někdo nějaké zavazadlo k převezení? dahl vahm <u>nyehg</u>·doh <u>nyeh</u>·yah·keh <u>zah</u>·vah·zah·dloh <u>kprzheh</u>·veh·zeh·nee	Did anyone give you anything to carry?
Vyndejte všechno z kapes, prosím. <u>vihn</u>·dehy·teh <u>fsheh</u>·khnoh z kah·pehs proh·seem	Please empty your pockets.
Zujte si boty, prosím. <u>zooy</u>·teh sih <u>boh</u>·tih proh·seem	Take off your shoes, please.
Zveme vás na palubu letadla... <u>zveh</u>·meh vahs nah <u>pah</u>·loo·boo <u>leh</u>·tahd·lah...	Now boarding flight...

Luggage

Where *is/are*...?	**Kde** *je/jsou*...? gdeh *yeh/ysoh*...
– the luggage carts [trolleys]	– **vozíky** <u>voh</u>·zee·kih
– the luggage lockers	– **schránky na zavazadla** <u>shrahn</u>·kih nah <u>zah</u>·vah·zahd·lah
– the baggage claim	– **výdej zavazadel** <u>vee</u>·dehy <u>zah</u>·vah·zah·dehl
My luggage has been lost.	**Ztratil♂/Ztratila♀ se mi zavazadla.** <u>strah</u>·tihl♂/<u>strah</u>·tih·lah♀ seh mih <u>zah</u>·vah·zah·dlah
My luggage has been stolen.	**Někdo mi ukradl zavazadla.** <u>nyehg</u>·doh mih <u>ook</u>·rahdl <u>zah</u>·vah·zah·dlah

| My suitcase was damaged. | **Můj kufr je poškozený.** mooy koofr yeh <u>poh</u>·shkoh·zeh·nee |

Finding Your Way

Where *is/are*...?	**Kde *je/jsou*...?** gdeh yeh/ysoh...
- the currency exchange office	- **směnárna** <u>smyeh</u>·nahr·nah
- the car rental [hire]	- **půjčovna aut** <u>pooy</u>·chohv·nah owt
- the exit	- **východ** <u>vee</u>·khohd
- the taxis	- **taxík** <u>tah</u>·kseek
Is there...into town?	**Jede do města...?** <u>yeh</u>·deh doh <u>myeh</u>·stah...
- a bus	- **autobusu** <u>ow</u>·toh·boo·soo
- a train	- **vlak** vlahk
- a subway [underground]	- **metro** <u>meh</u>·troh

▶ For directions, see page 31.

Train

How do I get to the train station?	**Jak se dostanu na nádraží?** yahk seh <u>doh</u>·stah·noo <u>nah</u>·nah·drah·zhee
Is it far?	**Je to daleko?** yeh toh <u>dah</u>·leh·koh
Where *is/are*...?	**Kde *je/jsou*...?** gdeh yeh/ysoh...
- the ticket office	- **pokladna** <u>poh</u>·klahd·nah
- the information desk	- **informace** <u>ihn</u>·fohr·mah·tseh
- the luggage lockers	- **schránky na zavazadla** <u>shrahn</u>·kih nah <u>zah</u>·vah·zah·dlah
- the platforms	- **nástupiště** <u>nah</u>·stoo·pihsh·tyeh

▶ For directions, see page 31.

▶ For ticketing, see page 18.

You May See...

K NÁSTUPIŠTÍM	to the platforms
INFORMACE	information
REZERVACE	reservations
PŘÍLETY	arrivals
ODLETY	departures

Questions

Could I have a schedule [timetable], please?	**Máte jízdní řád, prosím?** <u>mah</u>·teh <u>yeez</u>·dnee rzhaht <u>proh</u>·seem
How long is the trip [journey]?	**Jak dlouho trvá cesta?** yak <u>dloh</u>·hoh trfah <u>tsehs</u>·tah
Do I have to change trains?	**Musím přestupovat?** <u>moo</u>·seem <u>przheh</u>·stoo·poh·vaht

i

České dráhy (Czech state-owned railway) offers several transportation options. **Osobní vlak (Os)** (passenger train), stops at every station and operates usually from Monday to Friday, particularly in the morning and early afternoon. **Rychlík (R)** (express train), stops at selected stations, offers first and second class seating and sometimes also a **jídelní vůz** (restaurant car). **Intercity (IC)** and **Eurocity (EC)** ensure good traveling conditions: air-conditioned first- and second-class cars and a restaurant car. Night trains offer sleeping cars (first class) and couchettes (second class). Trains adapted for disabled persons and bicycles are specially marked.
Since not all ticket offices (especially in smaller towns) accept credit cards, it is advisable to have cash handy.

Departures

Which platform does the train to...leave from?	**Ze kterého nástupiště odjíždí vlak do...?** zeh kteh·reh·hoh nahs·too·pihsh·tyeh ohd·yeezh·dee vlahk doh...
Is this the track [platform] to...?	**Jede vlak do...z tohoto nástupiště?** yeh·deh vlahk do...stoh·hoh·toh nahs·too·pihsh·tyeh
Where is track [platform]...?	**Kde je...nástupiště?** gdeh yeh... nahs·too·pihsh·tyeh
Where do I change for...?	**Kde musím přestoupit na...?** gdeh moo·seem przheh·stoh·piht nah...

Boarding

Is this seat taken?	**Je tohle místo obsazeno?** yeh toh·hleh mees·toh ohp·sah·zeh·noh
I think that's my seat.	**Já myslím, že to je moje místo.** yah mihs·leem zheh toh yeh moh·yeh mees·toh

You May Hear...

Nastupujte prosím! nahs·too·pooy·teh proh·seem	All aboard!
Jízdenky, prosím. yeez·dehn·kih proh·seem	Tickets, please.
Musíte přestoupit v... moo·see·teh przheh·stoh·piht v...	You have to change at...
Příští zastávka... przheesh·tee zah·stahf·kah...	Next stop...

Bus

Where's the bus station?	**Kde je autobusové nádraží?** gdeh yeh ow·toh·boo·soh·veh nah·drah·zhee
How far is it?	**Jak je to daleko?** yahk yeh toh dah·leh·koh

How do I get to...?	**Jak se dostanu do...?** yahk seh <u>doh</u>·stah·noo doh...
Does the bus stop at...?	**Staví tenhle autobus v...?** <u>stah</u>·vee <u>tehn</u>·hle <u>ow</u>·toh·boos f...
Could you tell me when to get off?	**Můžete mi říct, kde mám vystoupit?** <u>moo</u>·zheh·teh mih rzheetst gdeh mahm vihs·toh·piht
Do I have to change buses?	**Musím přestupovat?** <u>moo</u>·seem <u>przhehs</u>·too·poh·vaht
Stop here, please!	**Zastavte tady, prosím!** <u>zahs</u>·stahf·teh <u>tah</u>·dih <u>proh</u>·seem

▶ For ticketing, see page 18.

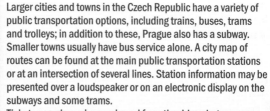

i Larger cities and towns in the Czech Republic have a variety of public transportation options, including trains, buses, trams and trolleys; in addition to these, Prague also has a subway. Smaller towns usually have bus service alone. A city map of routes can be found at the main public transportation stations or at an intersection of several lines. Station information may be presented over a loudspeaker or on an electronic display on the subways and some trams.

Tickets can always be purchased from the driver, but prepare the exact amount beforehand. Large cities often offer 24-hour tickets for use on all types of public transportation. Night service on buses and trams is available in major metropolitan areas; otherwise, hours of operation are generally 5 a.m. to 10.30 p.m.

You May See...

AUTOBUSOVÁ ZASTÁVKA	bus stop
VCHOD/VÝCHOD	enter/exit
ZDE OZNAČTE JÍZDENKU	stamp your ticket here

Subway [Underground]

Where's the nearest subway [underground] station?	**Kde je nejbližší stanice metra?** gdeh yeh <u>nehy</u>·blihzh·shee <u>stah</u>·nih·tseh <u>meht</u>·rah
Can I have a map of the subway [underground], please?	**Mohu dostat plán metra, prosím?** <u>moh</u>·hoo <u>dohs</u>·taht plahn <u>meht</u>·rah proh·seem
Which line for...?	**Kterou trasou se dostanu do...?** <u>kteh</u>·roh <u>trah</u>·soh seh <u>dohs</u>·tah·noo doh...
Where do I change for...?	**Kde musím přestoupit na...?** gdeh <u>moo</u>·seem <u>przheh</u>·stoh·piht nah...
Is this the right train for...?	**Jede to do...?** <u>yeh</u>·deh toh doh...
Where are we?	**Kde jsme?** gdeh ysmeh

▶ For ticketing, see page 18.

The Prague subway is comprised of three lines (A, B and C), and links to train stations and the Florenc bus station. You can change between lines at three stops: Muzeum (A and C lines), Můstek (A and B lines) and Florenc (B and C lines). The subway operates daily between 5 a.m. and midnight. During rush hour, trains arrive every 2–4 minutes; outside rush hour, every 4–10 minutes.

Boat

When is the boat to...?	**Kdy odplouvá loď na...?** gdih <u>ohd</u>·ploh·vah loh·dyeh <u>nah</u>...
Can I take my car on board?	**Mohu vzít na palubu svoje auto?** <u>moh</u>·hoo vzeet nah <u>pah</u>·loo·boo <u>sfo</u>·yeh <u>ow</u>·toh

▶ For ticketing, see page 18.

You May See...

ZÁCHRANNÝ ČLUN	life boats
ZÁCHRANNÁ VESTA	life jackets

 Though the Czech Republic is landlocked, cruising is popular along rivers and other bodies of water. There are several cruise locations, including Prague, Vltavě River, Lipno and Nové Mlýny dams and Máchovo lake.

Bicycle and Motorcycle

I'd like to rent...	**Chtěl♂/Chtěla♀ bych si půjčit...** khtyehl♂/khtyeh·lah♀ bihkh sih **pooy**·chiht...
– a bicycle	**– jízdní kolo** <u>yeez</u>·dnee <u>koh</u>·loh
– a moped	**– moped** <u>moh</u>·pehd
– a motorcycle	**– motorku** <u>moh</u>·tohr·koo
How much per day/week?	**Kolik to stojí na den/týden?** <u>koh</u>·lik toh <u>stoh</u>·yee nah dehn/<u>teeh</u>·den
Can I have a helmet/lock?	**Můžete mi dát přilbu/blokádu?** <u>moo</u>·zheh·teh mih daht <u>przhihl</u>·boo/<u>bloh</u>·<u>kah</u>·doo

Taxi

Where can I get a taxi?	**Kde najdu taxík?** gdeh <u>nahy</u>·doo <u>tah</u>·kseek
I'd like a taxi now/ for tomorrow at...	**Chtěl♂/Chtěla♀ bych taxík nyní/zítra v...** khtyehl♂/<u>khtyeh</u>·lah♀ bihkh <u>tah</u>·kseek <u>nih</u>·nee/<u>zeet</u>·rah f...
Please, pick me up at...	**Vyzvedněte mne, prosím, v...** <u>vihz</u>·vehd·nyeh·teh mneh <u>proh</u>·seem f...

Take me to...	**Zavezte mě laskavě na...** <u>zah</u>·vehs·teh myeh <u>lahs</u>·kah·vyeh nah...
- this address	**- tuhle adresu** <u>too</u>·hleh ahd·reh·soo
- the airport	**- letiště** <u>leh</u>·tihsh·tyeh
- the train station	**- nádraží** <u>nah</u>·drah·zhee
I'm late.	**Mám zpoždění.** mahm <u>spozh</u>·dyeh·nee
Can you drive *faster/slower*?	**Můžete jet *rychleji/pomaleji*?** <u>moo</u>·zheh·teh yeht <u>rih</u>·khleh·yih/<u>poh</u>·mah·leh·yih
Stop/Wait here.	**Zastavte/Počkejte zde.** <u>sah</u>·stahf·teh/<u>pohch</u>·kehy·teh sdeh
How much will it cost?	**Kolik to bude stát?** <u>koh</u>·lihk toh <u>boo</u>·deh staht
You said...crowns.	**Jste říkal...korun.** ysteh <u>rzhee</u>·kahl...<u>koh</u>·roon
Can I have a receipt?	**Mohli byste mi dát stvrzenku?** <u>moh</u>·hlih <u>bihs</u>·teh mih daht <u>stvrzehn</u>·koo
Keep the change.	**Nechte si drobné.** <u>nehkh</u>·teh sih <u>drohb</u>·neh

You May Hear...

Kam jedeme? kahm <u>yeh</u>·deh·meh	Where to?
Jaká adresa? <u>yah</u>·kah <u>ah</u>·dreh·sah	What's the address?

Taxi stands are marked with **TAXI** signs. Taxis can also be hailed in the street or reserved by phone. It is advisable to use the services of known taxi companies. These should post pricing information on the taxi door; the driver will have an ID. Ask for the estimated cost of the drive beforehand, and request a receipt if the pricing is higher once you arrive at your destination so that you can file a complaint. The form of payment should be established before departing. Tips are welcome and discretionary.

Car

Car Rental [Hire]

Where can I rent a car?	**Kde si mohu půjčit auto?** gdeh sih <u>moh</u>·hoo <u>pooy</u>·chiht <u>ow</u>·toh
I'd like to rent...	**Chtěl♂/Chtěla♀ bych si půjčit...** khtyehl♂/ <u>khtyeh</u>·lah♀ bihkh sih <u>pooy</u>·chiht...
– a 2-/4-door car	– **dvoudveřové/čtyřdveřové auto** <u>dvoh</u>·dveh·rzhoh·veh/<u>chtihrzh</u>·dveh·rzhoh·veh <u>ow</u>·toh
– an automatic	– **auto s automatickou převodovkou** <u>ow</u>·toh <u>sow</u>·toh·mah·tihts·koh <u>przheh</u>·voh·dohf·koh
– a car with air conditioning	– **auto s klimatizací** <u>ow</u>·toh <u>sklih</u>·mah·tih·zah·tsee
– a car seat	– **autosedačka** <u>ow</u>·toh·seh·dahch·kah
How much...?	**Kolik stojí...?** <u>koh</u>·lihk <u>stoh</u>·yee...
– per *day/week*	– **na *den/týden*** nah *dehn/<u>tee</u>·dehn*
– per kilometer	– **za kilometr** <u>zah</u>·kih·loh·mehtr
– for unlimited mileage	– **bez kilometrového limitu** behs <u>kih</u>·loh·meht·roh·veh·hoh <u>lih</u>·mih·tuh
– with insurance	– **s pojištěním** <u>spoh</u>·yihsh·tyeh·neem
Are there any discounts?	**Máte speciální slevy?** <u>mah</u>·teh <u>speh</u>·tsyahl·nee <u>sleh</u>·vih

You May Hear...

Pas, prosím. pahs <u>proh</u>·seem	Your passport, please.
Platí se záloha... <u>plah</u>·tee seh <u>zah</u>·loh·hah...	There is a deposit of...
Tady se podepište. <u>tah</u>·dih seh <u>poh</u>·deh·pihsh·teh	Sign here.

Gas [Petrol] Station

Where's the nearest gas [petrol] station, please?	**Kde je nejbližší benzínová pumpa, prosím?** gdeh yeh *nehy*·blihzh·shee *behn*·zee·noh·vah *poom*·pah proh·seem
Fill it up, please.	**Plnou nádrž, prosím.** plnoh nahdrzh proh·seem
...liters, please.	**...litrů, prosím.** ...*liht*·roo proh·seem
I'll pay *in cash/by credit card*.	**Zaplatím v hotovosti/kreditní kartou.** zah·plah·teem *fhoh*·toh·vohs·tih/*kreh*·diht·nee *kahr*·toh

You May See...

SPECIAL	regular
SUPER	premium [super]
NAFTA	diesel

Asking Directions

Is this the right road to...?	**Jedu správně na...?** yeh·doo sprah·vnyeh nah...
How far is it to...?	**Jak je to daleko do...?** yahk yeh toh *dah*·leh·koh doh...
Where's...?	**Kde je...?** gdeh yeh...
– ...Street	– **ulice...** *oo*·lih·tseh...
– this address	– **tuhle adresu** *too*·hleh *ahd*·reh·soo
– the highway [motorway]	– **dálnice** *dahl*·nih·tseh
Can you show me on the map?	**Můžete mi to ukázat na mapě?** *moo*·zheh·teh mih toh *oo*·kah·zaht *nah*·mah·pyeh
I'm lost.	**Ztratil♂/Ztratila♀ jsem se.** *strah*·tihl♂/ *strah*·tih·lah♀ ysehm seh

You May Hear...

přímo před vámi <u>przhee</u>·moh przhehd <u>vah</u>·mih	straight ahead
vlevo <u>vleh</u>·voh	on the left
vpravo <u>fprah</u>·voh	on the right
na rohu/za rohem nah <u>roh</u>·hoo/zah <u>roh</u>·hehm	*on/around* the corner
naproti... <u>nah</u>·proh·tih	opposite...
za... zah...	behind...
vedle... <u>vehd</u>·leh...	next to...
na sever/na jih <u>nah</u>·seh·vehr/<u>nah</u>·yihh	north/south
na východ/na západ <u>nah</u>·vee·khohd/<u>nah</u>·<u>zah</u>·pahd	east/west
na světlách <u>nah</u>·sfyeht·**lah**kh	at the traffic lights
na křižovatce na <u>krzhih</u>·zhoh·vaht·tseh	at the intersection

You May See...

STOP	**STŮJ**	stop
▽	**DEJ PŘEDNOST V JÍZDĚ**	yield
⊗	**ZÁKAZ STÁNÍ**	no parking
↑	**JEDNOSMĚRNÝ PROVOZ**	one way

	PRŮJEZD ZAKÁZÁN	no entry
	ZÁKAZ PŘEDJÍŽDĚNÍ	no passing
	PŘECHOD PRO CHODCE	pedestrian crossing

Parking

Can I park here?	**Můžu zde parkovat?** <u>moo</u>·zhoo zdeh pahr·koh·vaht	
Where is the nearest parking lot [car park]?	**Kde je nejbližší parkoviště?** gdeh yeh <u>nehy</u>·blihzh·shee pahr·koh·vihsh·tyeh	
How much...?	**Kolik...?** <u>koh</u>·lihk...	
- per hour	- **na hodinu** <u>nah</u>·hoh·dih·noo	
- per day	- **na den** <u>nah</u>·dehn	
- overnight	- **přes noc** przhehs nohts	

Breakdown and Repairs

My car broke down.	**Mám na autě poruchu.** mahm nah <u>ow</u>·tyeh poh·roo·khoo
My car won't start.	**Auto nechce nastartovat.** <u>ow</u>·toh nehkh·tseh <u>nah</u>·stahr·toh·vaht
Can you fix it?	**Můžete to opravit?** <u>moo</u>·zheh·teh toh <u>ohp</u>·rah·viht
When will it be ready?	**Kdy to bude hotové?** gdih toh <u>boo</u>·deh hoh·toh·veh
How much will it cost?	**Kolik to bude stát?** koh·lihk toh <u>boo</u>·deh staht

Accidents

There's been an accident.	**Stala se nehoda.** <u>stah</u>·lah seh <u>neh</u>·hoh·dah
Call *an ambulance/ the police.*	**Zavolejte *sanitku/policii.*** <u>zah</u>·voh·lehy·teh <u>sah</u>·niht·koo/<u>poh</u>·lih·tsih·yih

Accommodations

Essential

Can you recommend a hotel?	**Který hotel byste mi doporučil?** <u>kteh</u>·ree <u>hoh</u>·tehl <u>bihs</u>·teh mih <u>doh</u>·poh·roo·chihl
I have a reservation.	**Objednal♂/Objednala♀ jsem si pokoj.** <u>ohb</u>·yehd·nahl♂/<u>oh</u>·byehd·nah·lah♀ ysehm sih <u>poh</u>·kohy
My name is...	**Jmenuji se...** <u>ymeh</u>·noo·yih seh...
Do you have a room...?	**Máte volný pokoj...?** <u>mah</u>·teh <u>vohl</u>·nee <u>poh</u>·kohy...
– for *one/two*	– **jednolůžkový/dvoulůžkový** <u>yeh</u>·dnoh·<u>loozh</u>·koh·vee/<u>dvoh</u>·loozh·koh·vee
– with a bathroom	– **s koupelnou** <u>skoh</u>·pehl·noh
– with air conditioning	– **s klimatizací** <u>sklih</u>·mah·tih·zah·tsee
– for tonight	– **na jednu noc** <u>nah</u>·yehd·noo nots
– for two nights	– **na dvě noce** <u>nah</u>·dvyeh <u>noh</u>·tseh
– for one week	– **na týden** <u>nah</u>·tee·dehn
How much?	**Kolik?** <u>koh</u>·lihk
Do you have anything cheaper?	**Máte něco levnějšího?** <u>mah</u>·teh <u>nyeh</u>·tsoh <u>lehv</u>·nyehy·shee·hoh

When's check-out?	**V kolik hodin musíme uvolnit pokoj?** <u>fkoh</u>·lihk <u>hoh</u>·dihn <u>moo</u>·see·meh <u>oo</u>·vohl·niht <u>poh</u>·kohy
Can I leave this in the safe?	**Mohu tohle nechat v sejfu?** <u>moh</u>·hoo toh·hleh <u>neh</u>·khaht <u>fsehy</u>·foo
Can I leave my bags here?	**Mohu si zde nechat zavazadla?** <u>moh</u>·hoo sih zdeh <u>neh</u>·khaht <u>zah</u>·vah·zah·dlah
Can I have *the bill/a receipt*?	**Mohu dostat *stvrzenku/účet*?** <u>moh</u>·hoo dohs·taht <u>stvrzehn</u>·koo/<u>oo</u>·cheht
I'll pay *in cash/ by credit card*.	**Zaplatím *v hotovosti/kreditní kartou*.** zah·plah·teem *<u>fhoh</u>·toh·vohs·tih/<u>kreh</u>·diht·nee <u>kahr</u>·toh*

Finding Lodgings

Can you recommend a hotel?	**Který hotel byste mi doporučil?** kteh·ree <u>hoh</u>·tehl <u>bihs</u>·teh mih <u>doh</u>·poh·roo·chihl
What is it near to?	**Je někde nablízku?** yeh <u>nyehg</u>·deh <u>nah</u>·blee·skoo
How do I get there?	**Jak se tam dostanu?** yahk seh tahm <u>dohs</u>·tah·noo

The Czech Republic offers a large variety of accommodations, for every budget, ranging from five-star hotels to dormitory-style rooms in mountain hostels. For deluxe accommodations expect to pay high prices. Some of the best hotels in the country are located in former castles and palaces. Motels are found in the countryside and along the main highways; they are reasonably priced. Campsites are perfect for nature lovers. In the Czech Republic you'll find them along rivers and by lakes. Cabins need to be booked in advance, especially for summer months. **Privát** (private rooms) are equivalent to rooms in a bed and breakfast. Facilities vary. Hostels provide an alternative to inexpensive hotels. Dormitories are common and bathrooms are also shared. Their big advantage, though, is their location in historical city centers.

At the Hotel

I have a reservation.	**Objednal♂/Objednala♀ jsem si pokoj.** ohb·yehd·nahl♂/oh·byehd·nah·lah♀ ysehm sih poh·kohy
My name is...	**Jmenuji se...** ymeh·noo·yih seh...
Do you have a room...?	**Máte volný pokoj...?** mah·teh vohl·nee poh·kohy...
– with a *bathroom [toilet]/shower*	**– s *koupelnou/sprchou*** s koh·pehl·noh/ sprkhoh
– with air conditioning	**– s klimatizací** sklih·mah·tih·zah·tsee
– for tonight	**– na jednu noc** nah·yehd·noo nohts
– for two nights	**– na dvě noce** nah·dvyeh noh·tseh
– for one week	**– na týden** nah·tee·dehn
A *smoking/non-smoking room*, please.	**Pokoj pro *kuřáky/nekuřáky*, prosím.** poh·kohy proh *koo·rzhah·kih/neh·koo·rzhah·kih proh·seem*

▶ For numbers, see page 170.

Does the hotel have...?	**Je v hotelu...?** yeh fhoh·teh·loo...
– a computer	**– počítač** poh·chee·tahch
– an elevator [lift]	**– výtah** vee·tahh
– (wireless) internet service	**– (bezdrátové) internetové služby** (behz·drah·toh·veh) ihn·tehr·neh·toh·veh sloo·zhbih
– room service	**– room service** room sehr·vihs
– a gym	**– posilovna** poh·sih·loh·vnah
I need...	**Potřebuji...** poh·trzheh·boo·yih...
– an extra bed	**– lůžko navíc** loo·shkoh nah·veets

| – a cot | – **skládací postel** <u>sklah</u>·dah·tsee <u>pohs</u>·tehl |
| – a crib [child's cot] | – **kolébku** <u>koh</u>·lehp·koo |

You May Hear...

Váš cestovní pas/kreditní karta, prosím. vahsh <u>tsehs</u>·tohv·nee pahs/<u>kreh</u>·diht·nee <u>kahr</u>·tah <u>proh</u>·seem	Your *passport/ credit card*, please.
Vyplňte, prosím, tento formulář. <u>vih</u>·pln'teh <u>proh</u>·seem tehn·toh <u>fohr</u>·moo·lahrzh	Please fill out this form.
Tady se podepište. <u>tah</u>·dih seh <u>poh</u>·deh·pihsh·the	Sign here.

Price

| How much per *night/week*? | **Kolik se platí za *noc/týden*?** <u>koh</u>·lihk seh <u>plah</u>·tee zah *nohts/<u>tee</u>·dehn* |
| Does the price include *breakfast/ sales tax [VAT]*? | **Je v ceně *snídaně/DPH*?** yeh <u>ftseh</u>·nyeh *<u>snee</u>·dah·nyeh/<u>deh</u>·peh·hah* |

Questions

Where's...?	**Kde je...?** gdeh yeh...
– the bar	– **bar** bahr
– the elevator [lift]	– **výtah** <u>vee</u>·tahh
– the restroom [toilet]	– **záchod** <u>zah</u>·khoht
Can I have...?	**Mohu dostat...?** <u>moh</u>·hoo <u>dohs</u>·taht...
– a blanket	– **přikrývku** <u>przhih</u>·kreef·koo
– an iron	– **žehličku** <u>zheh</u>·hlihch·koo
– a pillow	– **polštář** <u>pohlsh</u>·tahrzh
– soap	– **mýdlo** <u>mee</u>·dloh

Can I have...?	**Mohu dostat...?** <u>moh</u>·hoo <u>dohs</u>·taht...
– toilet paper	**– toaletní papír** <u>toh</u>·ah·leht·nee pah·peer
– a towel	**– ručník** <u>rooch</u>·neek
Do you have an adapter for this?	**Máte k tomu adapteru?** <u>mah</u>·teh <u>ktoh</u>·moo <u>ah</u>·dahp·teh·<u>roo</u>
How do I turn on the lights?	**Jak se zde zapíná svetlo?** yahk seh zdeh <u>zah</u>·pee·nah <u>sveht</u>·loh
Could you wake me at...?	**Vzbudili byste mě v...?** <u>vzboo</u>·dih·lih <u>bihs</u>·teh myeh f...

▶ For time, see page 172.

| I'd like my things from the safe. | **Chtěl♂/Chtěla♀ bych si vyzvednout své věci ze sejfu.** khtyehl♂/<u>khtyeh</u>·lah♀ bihkh sih <u>vihz</u>·vehd·noht sfeh <u>vyeh</u>·tsih <u>zeh</u>·sehy·foo |
| Is there *mail/ a message* for me? | **Máte pro mne *nějakou poštu/nějaký vzkaz?*** <u>mah</u>·teh proh mneh <u>nyeh</u>·jah·koh <u>pohsh</u>·too/ <u>nyeh</u>·yah·**kee** fskahz |

You May See...

TAM/SEM	push/pull
ZÁCHODY	restroom [toilet]
SPRCHA	shower
VÝTAH	elevator [lift]
SCHODIŠTĚ	stairs
PRÁDELNÍ SLUŽBA	laundry
NERUŠIT	do not disturb
PROTIPOŽÁRNÍ DVEŘE	fire door
NOUZOVÝ VÝCHOD	emergency exit
BUZENÍ TELEFONEM	wake-up call

Problems

There's a problem.	**Mám problém.** mahm <u>prohb</u>·lehm
I've lost my *key/key card*.	**Ztratil**♂/**Ztratila**♀ **jsem** *klíč/klíčovú kartu.* <u>strah</u>·tihl♂/<u>strah</u>·tih·lah♀ ysehm *kleech/ klee·choh·voo <u>kahr</u>·too*
I've locked myself out of my room.	**Zabouchl**♂/**Zabouchla**♀ **jsem si dveře.** zah·bohkhl♂/<u>zah</u>·boh·khlah♀ ysehm sih <u>dveh</u>·rzheh
There's no hot water.	**Neteče horká voda.** <u>neh</u>·teh·cheh <u>hohr</u>·kah <u>voh</u>·dah
There's no toilet paper.	**Není tam toaletní papír.** <u>neh</u>·nee tahm <u>toh</u>·ah·leht·nee <u>pah</u>·peer
The room is dirty.	**Pokoj je špinavý.** <u>poh</u>·kohy yeh <u>shpih</u>·nah·vee
There are bugs in our room.	**V našem pokoji jsou hmyzy.** <u>vnah</u>·shehm <u>poh</u>·koh·yih yhsoh <u>hmih</u>·zih
...doesn't work.	**...nefunguje.** ...<u>neh</u>·foon·goo·yeh
Can you fix...?	**Můžete opravit...?** <u>moo</u>·zheh·teh <u>oh</u>·prah·viht...
– the air conditioning	– **klimatizace** <u>klih</u>·mah·tih·zah·tseh
– the fan	– **větrák** <u>vyeht</u>·rahk

Can you fix...?	**Můžete opravit...?** <u>moo</u>·zheh·teh <u>oh</u>·prah·viht...
- the heat [heating]	- **topení** <u>toh</u>·peh·nee
- the light	- **světlo** <u>svyeht</u>·loh
- the TV	- **TV** <u>tih</u>·vih
- the toilet	- **záchod** <u>zah</u>·khohd
I'd like to move to another room.	**Chtěl♂/Chtěla♀ bych se přestěhovat do jiného pokoje.** khtyehl♂/<u>khtyeh</u>·lah♀ bihkh seh <u>przheh</u>·styeh·hoh·vaht doh <u>yih</u>·neh·hoh <u>poh</u>·koh·yeh

Electricity in the Czech Republic is 230 volts. You may need a converter and/or an adapter for your appliances.

Check-out

When's check-out?	**V kolik hodin musíme uvolnit pokoj?** <u>fkoh</u>·lihk hoh·dihn <u>moo</u>·see·meh <u>oo</u>·vohl·niht <u>poh</u>·kohy
Could I leave my bags here until...?	**Mohu si tady nechat zavazadla doh...?** <u>moh</u>·hoo sih <u>tah</u>·dih neh·khaht <u>zah</u>·vah·zah·dlah doh...
Can I have an *itemized bill/ a receipt*?	**Mohli byste mi *účet rozepsat/dát stvrzenku*?** <u>moh</u>·hlih bihs·teh mih <u>oo</u>·cheht <u>roh</u>·zehp·saht/<u>daht stvrzehn</u>·koo
I think there's a mistake in this bill.	**Myslím, že v účtu je chyba.** <u>mihs</u>·leem zheh <u>voo</u>·chtoo yeh <u>khih</u>·bah
I'll pay *in cash/by credit card*.	**Zaplatím *v hotovosti/kreditní kartou*.** <u>zah</u>·plah·teem *<u>fhoh</u>·toh·vohs·tih/<u>kreh</u>·diht·nee <u>kar</u>·toh*

Hotel staff (doormen, porters and housekeeping personnel) are customarily tipped a few **korun** for service.

Renting

I've reserved *an apartment/a room*.	**Objednal♂/Objednala♀ jsem si u vás *byt/pokoj.*** <u>ohb</u>·yehd·nahl♂/<u>ohb</u>·yehd·nah·lah♀ ysehm sih oo vahs *biht/<u>poh</u>·kohy*
My name is...	**Jmenuji se...** <u>ymeh</u>·noo·yih seh...
Can I have the *key/key card*?	**Mohu dostat *klíč/klíčovú kartu*?** <u>moh</u>·hoo <u>dohs</u>·taht *kleech/<u>klee</u>·choh·voo <u>kahr</u>·too*
Are there sheets?	**Je zde ložní prádlo?** yeh zdeh <u>lohzh</u>·nee <u>prah</u>·dloh
Are there...?	**Jsou zde...?** ysoh zdeh...
– dishes	– **nádobí** <u>nah</u>·doh·bee
– pillows	– **polštáře** <u>pohl</u>·shtah·rzheh
– towels	– **ručníky** <u>rooch</u>·nee·kih
When/Where do I put out the trash [rubbish]?	***Kdy/Kam* odvážejí odpadky?** gdih/kahm <u>ohd</u>·vah·zheh·yee <u>ohd</u>·pahd·kih
...is broken.	**...nefunguje.** ...<u>neh</u>·foon·goo·yeh
How does...work?	**Jak...funguje?** yahk...<u>foon</u>·goo·yeh
– the air conditioner	– **klimatizace** <u>klih</u>·mah·tih·zah·tseh
– the dishwasher	– **myčka** <u>mihch</u>·kah
– the freezer	– **mraznička** <u>mrahz</u>·nihch·kah
– the heater	– **topení** <u>toh</u>·peh·nee
– the microwave	– **mikrovlnná trouba** <u>mih</u>·kroh·vlnah <u>troh</u>·bah
– the refrigerator	– **lednička** <u>lehd</u>·nihch·kah
– the stove	– **vařič** <u>vah</u>·rzhihch
– the washing machine	– **pračka** <u>prahch</u>·kah

▶ For oven temperatures, see page 175.

Household Items

I need...	Potřebuji... poh·trzheh·boo·yih...
– an adapter	– **adaptér** <u>ah</u>·dahp·tehr
– aluminum [kitchen] foil	– **alobal** <u>ah</u>·loh·bahl
– a bottle opener	– **otvírač na láhve** <u>oht</u>·fee·rahch <u>nah</u>·lah·hveh
– a broom	– **smetáček** <u>smeh</u>·tah·chehk
– a can opener	– **otvírač na plechovky** <u>oht</u>·fee·rahch <u>nah</u>·pleh·khohf·kih
– cleaning supplies	– **čisticí potřeby** <u>chihs</u>·tih·tsee <u>poht</u>·rzheh·bih
– a corkscrew	– **vývrtku** <u>vee</u>·vrtkoo
– detergent	– **prášek na praní** <u>prah</u>·shehk <u>nah</u>·prah·nee
– dishwashing liquid	– **prostředek na mytí nádobí** <u>prohs</u>·trzheh·dehk <u>nah</u>·mih·tee <u>nah</u>·doh·bee
– garbage [rubbish] bags	– **pytle na odpadky** <u>piht</u>·leh <u>nah</u>·oht·paht·kih
– a light bulb	– **žárovku** <u>zhah</u>·rohf·koo
– matches	– **zápalky** <u>zah</u>·pahl·kih
– a mop	– **mop** mohp
– napkins	– **papírové ubrousky** <u>pah</u>·pee·roh·veh <u>oob</u>·rohs·kih
– paper towels	– **papírové ručníky** <u>pah</u>·pee·roh·veh <u>rooch</u>·nee·kih
– plastic wrap [cling film]	**potravinovou fólii** <u>poht</u>·rah·vih·noh·voh <u>foh</u>·lyih
– a plunger	– **plunžr** ploonzhr
– scissors	– **nůžky** <u>noosh</u>·kih
– a vacuum cleaner	– **vysavač** <u>vih</u>·sah·vahch

► For dishes and utensils, see page 62.

Hostel

Do you have any places left for tonight?	**Máte na dnes ještě volná místa?** <u>mah</u>·teh <u>nah</u>·dnehs <u>yehsh</u>·tyeh <u>vohl</u>·nah <u>mees</u>·tah
Can I have...?	**Mohu dostat...?** <u>moh</u>·hoo <u>dohs</u>·taht...
– a *single/double* room	– *jednolůžkový/dvoulůžkový pokoj* <u>yehd</u>·noh·<u>loo</u>zh·koh·vee/<u>dvoh</u>·<u>loo</u>zh·koh·vee <u>poh</u>·kohy
– a blanket	– **přikrývku** <u>przhih</u>·kreef·koo
– pillows	– **polštáře** <u>pohl</u>·shtah·rzheh
– sheets	– **ložní prádlo** <u>lohzh</u>·nee <u>prah</u>·dloh
– towels	– **ručníky** <u>rooch</u>·nee·kih
What time do you lock up?	**V kolik hodin se zamyká vchod?** <u>fkoh</u>·lihk <u>hoh</u>·dihn seh <u>zah</u>·mih·kah fkhoht

Youth hostels are popular in the Czech Republic. They usually offer both private and dormitory-style rooms. Being relatively inexpensive, they attract mainly young people and budget travelers. Additional budget accommodations are available; try **vysokoškolské koleje** (university dorms, especially in the summer) and **ubytovny** (cheap group accommodation facilities). Although their standard is not high (multiple dorms, shared bathroom facilities), the price per bed is very low.

Camping

Can I camp here?	**Mohu tady postavit stan?** <u>moh</u>·hoo <u>tah</u>·dih <u>pohs</u>·tah·viht stahn
Is there a campsite near here?	**Je tu nablízku kempink?** yeh too <u>nah</u>·blees·koo <u>kehm</u>·pihnk
What is the charge per *day/week*?	**Jaký je poplatek za *den/týden*?** <u>yah</u>·kee yeh <u>poh</u>·plah·tehk zah *dehn/<u>tee</u>·dehn*

Are there...?	Je zde...? yeh zdeh...
- cooking facilities	- **kuchyňské vybavení** <u>koo</u>·khihn'·skeh <u>vih</u>·bah·veh·**nee**
- electrical outlets	- **elektrické zásuvky** <u>eh</u>·lehk·trihts·keh <u>zah</u>·soof·kih
- laundry facilities	- **prádelna** <u>prah</u>·dehl·nah
- showers	- **sprchy** sprkhih
- tents for rent [hire]	- **možnost si vypůjčit stan** <u>mohzh</u>·nohst sih <u>vih</u>·**pooy**·chiht stahn
Where can I empty the chemical toilet?	**Kde můžu vyprázdnit chemický záchod?** gdeh <u>moo</u>·zhoo <u>vihp</u>·rahzd·niht <u>kheh</u>·mihts·kee <u>zah</u>·khohd

▶ For household items, see page 42.

▶ For dishes and utensils, see page 62.

You May See...

PITNÁ VODA	drinking water
ZÁKAZ KEMPOVÁNÍ	no camping
ZÁKAZ ROZDĚLÁVÁNÍ OHNĚ/POUŽITÍ GRILU	no fires/barbecues

Internet and Communications

Essential

Is there an internet café nearby?	**Je tady někde nablízku internetová kavárna?** yeh <u>tah</u>·dih <u>nyeg</u>·deh <u>na</u>·blees·kuh ihn·tehr·neh·toh·vah <u>kah</u>·vahr·nah

Can I *access the internet/check e-mail* here?	**Mohu zde *použit internet/přečíst poštu*?** moh·hoo zdeh *poh·zhiht ihn·tehr·neht/ przheh·cheest pohsh·too*
How much per *hour/half hour*?	**Kolik stojí *hodina/půl hodiny*?** koh·lihk stoh·yee *hoh·dih·nah/pool hoh·dih·nih*
How do I *connect/ log on*?	**Jak se mohu *připojit na síť/zalogovat*?** yahk seh moh·hoo *przhih·poh·yiht nah seet'/ zah·loh·goh·vaht*
I'd like a phone card.	**Chtěl♂/Chtěla♀ bych telefonní kartu.** khtyehl♂/khtyeh·lah♀ bihkh teh·leh·fohn·nee kahr·too
Can I have your phone number?	**Dáte mi vaše telefonní číslo?** dah·teh mih vah·sheh teh·leh·fohn·nee chees·loh
Here's my *number/ e-mail address*.	**Tady je moje *číslo/emailová adresa*.** tah·dih yeh moh·yeh *chees·loh/eh·mehy·loh·vah ahd·reh·sah*
Call me.	**Zavolejte mi.** zah·voh·lehy·teh mih
E-mail me.	**Pošlete mi e-mail.** poh·shleh·teh mih eh·mehyl
Hello. This is...	**Dobrý den. Tady je...** dohb·ree dehn tah·dih yeh...
I'd like to speak to...	**Chtěl♂/Chtěla♀ bych mluvit s...** khtyehl♂/ khtyeh·lah♀ bihkh mloo·viht s...
Could you repeat that?	**Můžete to zopakovat?** moo·zheh·teh toh zoh·pah·koh·vaht
I'll call back later.	**Zavolám později.** zah·voh·lahm pohz·dyeh·yih
Bye.	**Na shledanou.** nahs·hleh·dah·noh
Where's the post office?	**Kde je pošta?** gdeh yeh pohsh·tah
I'd like to send this to...	**Chtěl♂/Chtěla♀ bych to poslat do...** khtyehl♂/khtyeh·lah♀ bihkh toh pohs·laht doh...

Computer, Internet and E-mail

Where's an internet cafe?	**Kde je internetová kavárna?** gdeh yeh <u>ihn</u>·tehr·neh·toh·**vah** kah·<u>vahr</u>·nah
Does it have wireless internet?	**Je tady bezdrátový internet?** yeh <u>tah</u>·dih <u>behz</u>·drah·toh·vee <u>ihn</u>·tehr·neht
How do I turn the computer on/off?	**Jak se zapíná/vypíná počítač?** yahk seh <u>zah</u>·pee·nah/<u>vih</u>·pee·nah poh·chee·tahch
Can I...?	**Mohu...?** <u>moh</u>·hoo...
– access the internet here	– **se odtud připojit na internet** seh <u>oht</u>·tood <u>przhih</u>·poh·yiht nah·ihn·tehr·neht
– check e-mail	– **skontrolovat poštu** <u>skohn</u>·troh·loh·vaht <u>pohsh</u>·too
– print	– **něco vytisknout** <u>nyeh</u>·tsoh <u>vih</u>·tihs·knoht
– use any computer	– **používat počítač** <u>poh</u>·oo·zhee·vaht <u>poh</u>·chee·tahch

How do I...?	**Jak se mohu...?** yahk seh <u>moh</u>·hoo...
– connect/ disconnect	– **připojit na síť/odpojit** <u>przhih</u>·poh·yiht nah seet'/<u>oht</u>·poh·yeet
– log *on/off*	– **zalogovat/vylogovat** <u>zah</u>·loh·goh·vaht/ <u>vih</u>·loh·goh·vaht
– type this symbol	– **zapsat tento symbol** <u>zahp</u>·saht <u>tehn</u>·toh <u>sihm</u>·bohl
How much per *hour/half hour*?	**Kolik stojí *hodina/půl hodiny*?** <u>koh</u>·lihk <u>stoh</u>·yee <u>hoh</u>·dih·nah/pool <u>hoh</u>·dih·nih
What's your e-mail?	**Jakou máte emailovou adresu?** <u>yah</u>·koh <u>mah</u>·teh <u>eh</u>·mehy·loh·voh <u>ahd</u>·reh·soo
My e-mail is...	**Moje emailová adresa je...** <u>moh</u>·yeh <u>eh</u>·mehy·loh·**vah** <u>ahd</u>·reh·sah yeh...

You May See...

ZAVŘIT	close
ZRUŠIT	delete
E-MAIL	e-mail
UKONČIT	exit
POMOC	help
KOMUNIKÁTOR	instant messenger
INTERNET	internet
LOGIN	login
NOVÝ VZKAZ	new (message)
ZALOGOVAT/VYLOGOVAT	log *on/off*
OTEVŘIT	open
TISKNOUT	print

CHRÁNIT	save
POSLAT	send
NÁZEV UŽIVATELE/HESLO	username/ password
BEZDRÁTOVÝ INTERNET	wireless internet

Phone

A phone card, please.
Kartu na telefon, prosím. kahr·too nah·teh·leh·fohn proh·seem

How much?
Kolik? koh·lihk

My phone doesn't work here.
Můj telefon zde nefunguje. mooy teh·leh·fohn zdeh neh·foon·goo·yeh

What's the country code for...?
Jaké je směrovací číslo do...? yah·keh yeh smyeh·roh·vah·tsee chee·sloh doh...

What's the number for Information?	**Jake je číslo na informaci?** <u>yah</u>·keh yeh <u>chee</u>·sloh nah <u>ihn</u>·fohr·mah·tsih
I'd like the number for...	**Chtěl♂/Chtěla♀ bych číslo na...** khtyehl♂/<u>khtyeh</u>·lah♀ bihkh <u>chee</u>·sloh nah...
Can I have your number?	**Dáte mi vaše telefonní číslo?** <u>dah</u>·teh mih <u>vah</u>·sheh <u>teh</u>·leh·foh·nee <u>chees</u>·loh
Here's my number.	**Tady je moje číslo.** <u>tah</u>·dih yeh <u>moh</u>·yeh <u>chees</u>·loh

▶ For numbers, see page 170.

Call me.	**Zavolejte mi.** <u>zah</u>·voh·lehy·teh mih
Text me.	**Pošlete mi sms-ku.** <u>pohsh</u>·leh·teh mih ehs·ehm·ehs·koo
I'll call you.	**Zavolám vás.** <u>zah</u>·voh·lahm vahs
I'll text you.	**Pošlu vám sms-ku.** <u>pohsh</u>·loo vahm ehs·ehm·ehs·koo

On the Phone

Hello. This is...	**Dobrý den. Tady je...** <u>dohb</u>·ree dehn <u>tah</u>·dih yeh...
I'd like to speak to...	**Chtěl♂/Chtěla♀ bych mluvit s...** khtyehl♂/<u>khtyeh</u>·lah♀ bihkh <u>mloo</u>·viht s...
Extension...	**Linka...** <u>lihn</u>·kah...
Speak *louder/more slowly*, please.	**Mluvte *hlasitěji/pomaleji*, prosím.** <u>mloof</u>·teh <u>hlah</u>·sih·tyeh·yih/<u>poh</u>·mah·leh·yih <u>proh</u>·seem
Could you repeat that?	**Můžete to zopakovat?** <u>moo</u>·zheh·teh toh <u>zoh</u>·pah·koh·vaht
I'll call back later.	**Zavolám později.** <u>zah</u>·voh·lahm <u>pohz</u>·dyeh·yih
Bye.	**Na shledanou.** <u>nahs</u>·hleh·dah·noh

▶ For business travel, see page 143.

You May Hear...

Promiňte, kdo volá? <u>proh</u>·meen'·tyeh gdoh <u>voh</u>·lah	Who's calling, please?
Počkejte chvilku, prosím. pohch·kehy·teh <u>khfihl</u>·koo proh·seem	Hold, please.
Přepojím Vás. <u>przheh</u>·poh·yeem vahs	I'll put you through.
Bohužel *on/ona* tady není. <u>boh</u>·hoo·zhehl ohn/<u>oh</u>·nah <u>tah</u>·dih <u>neh</u>·nee	I'm afraid *he/she* is not in.
Bohužel, teď to *on/ona* nemůže vzít. <u>boh</u>·hoo·zhehl tehdy toh ohn/<u>oh</u>·nah neh·**moo**·zheh vzeet	I'm afraid *he/she* can't come to the phone.
Chcete jí nechat vzkaz? <u>khtseh</u>·teh yih neh·khaht fskahs	Would you like to leave a message?
Zavolejte *později/za deset minut*. zah·voh·lehy·teh <u>pohz</u>·dyeh·yih/zah <u>deh</u>·seht <u>mih</u>·noot	Call back *later/ in 10 minutes*.
Může vám *on/ona* zavolat? <u>moo</u>·zheh vahm ohn/<u>oh</u>·nah <u>zah</u>·voh·laht	Can *he/she* call you back?
Jaké je vaše číslo? <u>yah</u>·keh yeh <u>vah</u>·sheh <u>chee</u>·sloh	What's your number?

Fax ────────────────────────

Can I *send/receive* a fax here?	**Můžu *odtud odeslat/zde prijmout* fax?** <u>moo</u>·zhoo <u>ohd</u>·tood <u>oh</u>·dehs·laht/zdeh <u>prihy</u>·moht fahks
What's the fax number?	**Jaké je číslo faxu?** <u>yah</u>·keh yeh <u>chee</u>·sloh <u>fahk</u>·soo
Please fax this to...	**Přefaxujte mi to, prosím, do...** <u>przheh</u>·fah·ksooy·teh mih toh <u>proh</u>·seem doh...

50

Post Office

Where's the *post office/mailbox [postbox]*?	**Kde je *pošta/poštovní schránka*?** gdeh yeh *pohsh·tah/pohsh·tohv·nee shrahn·kah*
A stamp for *postcard/letter*, please.	**Známku na *pohlednici/dopis*, prosím.** *znahm·koo nah poh·hlehd·nih·tsih/doh·pihs proh·seem*
How much?	**Kolik?** koh·lihk
I want to send this package by *airmail/express*.	**Chtel♂/Chtěla♀ bych poslat tento balík *letecky/spěšně*.** khtyehl♂/khtyeh·lah♀ bihkh pohs·laht tehn·toh bah·leek leh·tehts·kih/spyehsh·nyeh
A receipt, please.	**Stvrzenku, prosím.** stvrzehn·koo proh·seem

You May Hear...

Vyplňte laskavě celní prohlášení. vihplnʼ·teh lahs·kah·vyeh tsehl·nee proh·hlah·sheh·nee	Please fill out the customs declaration form.
Jakou má hodnotu? yah·koh mah hohd·noh·too	What's the value?
Co v něm je? tsoh vnyehm yeh	What's inside?

Hours of operation for **pošty** (post offices) are: Monday to Friday, 8 a.m. to 5 or 6 p.m. with a one-hour break around noon; Saturday, 8 a.m. to noon. In large cities, such as Ostrava or Brno, some post offices have longer hours, while the main post office in Prague is open 24-hours a day, seven days a week. Post offices can also be found at some shopping malls.

▼ Food

Essential

Can you recommend a good *restaurant/bar*?	**Můžete mi doporučit dobrou *restauraci/ bar*?** <u>moo</u>·zheh·teh mih <u>doh</u>·poh·roo·chiht <u>doh</u>·broh <u>rehs</u>·tow·rah·tsih/bahr
Is there a traditional Czech/ an inexpensive restaurant near here?	**Je tu někde nablízku *tradiční česká/levná* restaurace?** yeh too <u>nyek</u>·deh <u>nahb</u>·lees·koo <u>trah</u>·dihch·nee chehs·kah/<u>lehv</u>·nah rehs·tow·rah·tseh
A table for..., please.	**Stůl pro..., prosím.** stool proh...<u>proh</u>·seem
Could we sit...?	**Mohli bychom si sednout...?** <u>moh</u>·hlih bih·khohm sih <u>sehd</u>·noht...
– here/there	**– tady/tam** <u>tah</u>·dih/tahm
– outside	**– venku** <u>vehn</u>·koo
– in a non-smoking area	**– v části pro nekuřáky** <u>fchahs</u>·tih proh neh·koo·rzhah·kih
I'm waiting for someone.	**Čekám někoho.** <u>cheh</u>·kahm <u>nyeh</u>·koh·hoh
Where are the restrooms [toilets]?	**Kde jsou záchody?** gdeh ysoh <u>zah</u>·khoh·dih
A menu, please.	**Jídelní lístek, prosím.** <u>yee</u>·dehl·nee <u>lees</u>·tehk <u>proh</u>·seem
What do you recommend?	**Co nám můžete doporučit?** tsoh nahm <u>moo</u>·zheh·the <u>doh</u>·poh·roo·chiht
I'd like...	**Chtěl♂/Chtěla♀ bych...** khtyehl♂/ <u>khtyeh</u>·lah♀ bikh...
Some more..., please.	**Ještě trochu..., prosím.** <u>yehsh</u>·tyeh <u>troh</u>·khoo...<u>proh</u>·seem
Enjoy your meal.	**Nechte si chutnat.** <u>nehkh</u>·teh sih <u>khoot</u>·naht

The check [bill], please.	**Účet, prosím.** oo·cheht proh·seem
Is service included?	**Je v tom zahrnutá obsluha?** yeh ftohm zah·hrnoo·tah ohp·sloo·hah
Can I pay by credit card?	**Mohu zaplatit kreditní kartou?** moh·hoo zah·plah·tiht kreh·diht·nee kahr·toh
Can I have a receipt?	**Mohu dostat stvrzenku?** moh·hoo dohs·taht stvrzehn·koo
Thank you.	**Děkuji.** dyeh·koo·yih

Restaurant Types

Can you recommend...?	**Můžete mi doporučit...?** moo·zheh·teh mih doh·poh·roo·chiht...
– a restaurant	– **restauraci** rehs·tow·rah·tsih
– a bar	– **bar** bahr
– a cafe	– **bufet** boo·feht
– a fast-food place	– **rychlé občerstvení** rihkh·leh ohp·chehrs·tfeh·nee

Reservations and Questions

I'd like to reserve a table...	**Chtěl♂/Chtěla♀ bych si objednat stůl...** khtyehl♂/khtyeh·lah♀ bihkh sih ohb·yehd·naht stoohl...
– for two	– **pro dva** proh dvah
– for this evening	– **na dnes večer** nah·dnehs veh·chehr
– for tomorrow at...	– **na zítra na...** nah·zeet·rah nah...
A table for two, please.	**Stůl pro dva, prosím.** stoohl proh dvah proh·seem
We have a reservation.	**Máme tu rezervaci.** mah·meh too reh·zehr·vah·tsih

My name is...	**Jmenuji se...** <u>ymeh</u>·noo·yih seh...
Could we sit...?	**Mohli bychom si sednout...?** <u>moh</u>·lih <u>bih</u>·khohm sih <u>sehd</u>·noht
– here/there	– **tady/tam** <u>tah</u>·dih/tahm
– outside	– **venku** <u>vehn</u>·koo
– in a non-smoking area	– **v části pro nekuřáky** <u>fchahs</u>·tih proh neh·koo·rzh**ah**·kih
– by the window	– **u okna** <u>oo</u>·ohk·nah
Where are the restrooms [toilets]?	**Kde jsou záchody?** gdeh ysoh <u>zah</u>·khoh·dih

You May Hear...

Máte rezervaci? <u>mah</u>·teh <u>reh</u>·zehr·vah·tsih	Do you have a reservation?
Kolik osob? <u>koh</u>·lihk <u>oh</u>·sohp	How many people?
Pro kuřáky nebo nekuřáky? <u>proh</u>·koo·rzh**ah**·kih <u>neh</u>·boh <u>neh</u>·koo·rzh**ah**·kih	Smoking or non-smoking?
Chcete si objednat? <u>khtseh</u>·teh sih <u>oh</u>·byehd·naht	Are you ready to order?
Co byste si přáli? tsoh <u>bih</u>·styeh sih <u>przhah</u>·lih	What would you like?
Doporučil bych... <u>doh</u>·poh·roo·chihl bihkh...	I recommend...
Dobrou chuť. <u>doh</u>·broh khoot'	Enjoy your meal.

Ordering

Waiter/Waitress!	**Pane vrchní/Paní vrchní!** <u>pah</u>·neh vrkhnee/ <u>pah</u>·nee vrkhnee
We're ready to order.	**Chtěli bychom si objednat.** <u>khtyeh</u>·lih <u>bih</u>·khohm sih <u>ohb</u>·yehd·naht

May I see the drink menu?	**Mohl**♂/**Mohla**♀ **bych vidět nápojový lístek?** mohl♂/<u>moh</u>·hlah♀ bihkh <u>vih</u>·dyeht <u>nah</u>·poh·yoh·vee <u>lees</u>·tehk
I'd like...	**Chtěl**♂/**Chtěla**♀ **bych...** khtyehl♂/ khtyeh·lah♀ bikh...
– a bottle of...	– **láhev...** <u>lah</u>·hehf...
– a carafe of...	– **džbánek...** <u>dzhbah</u>·nehk...
– a glass of...	– **sklenici...** <u>skleh</u>·nih·tsih...

▶ For alcoholic and non-alcoholic drinks, see page 72.

The menu, please.	**Jídelní lístek, prosím.** <u>yee</u>·dehl·nee <u>lees</u>·tehk <u>proh</u>·seem
Do you have...?	**Máte...?** <u>mah</u>·teh...
– a menu in English	– **jídelní lístek v angličtině** <u>yee</u>·dehl·nee <u>lees</u>·tehk <u>vahng</u>·lihch·tih·nyeh
– a fixed-price menu	– **polední menu** <u>poh</u>·lehd·nee <u>meh</u>·nih
– a children's menu	– **jídelníček pro děti** <u>yee</u>·dehl·nee·chehk proh <u>dyeh</u>·tih

What do you recommend?	**Co byste mi doporučil?** tsoh <u>bih</u>·steh mih <u>doh</u>·poh·roo·chihl
What's this?	**Co to je?** tsoh toh yeh
What's in it?	**Z čeho to je?** <u>scheh</u>·hoh toh yeh
Is it spicy?	**Je to pikantní?** yeh toh <u>pih</u>·kahnt·nee
It's to go [take away].	**Vezmu si to s sebou.** <u>vehz</u>·moo sih toh <u>sseh</u>·boh

You May See...

JÍDELNÍ LÍSTEK	menu
NABÍDKA DNE	menu of the day
KUVERT A SERVIS (NENÍ) V CENĚ JÍDLA	cover charge and service (not) included in price

Cooking Methods

baked	**pečené** <u>peh</u>·cheh·neh
boiled	**vařené** <u>vah</u>·rzheh·neh
braised	**dušené** <u>doo</u>·sheh·neh
breaded	**ve strouhance** <u>veh</u>·stroh·hahn·tseh
creamed	**ve smetaně** <u>veh</u>·smeh·tah·nyeh
diced	**nakrájené na kostičky** <u>nah</u>·krah·yeh·neh <u>nah</u>·kohs·tihch·kih
fileted	**filé** <u>fih</u>·leh
fried	**smažené** <u>smah</u>·zheh·neh
grilled	**grilované** <u>grih</u>·loh·vah·neh
poached	**z vody** <u>sfoh</u>·dih
roasted	**pečené** <u>peh</u>·cheh·neh
sautéed	**na másle** <u>nah</u>·mah·sleh
smoked	**uzené** <u>oo</u>·zheh·neh
steamed	**dušené v páře** <u>doo</u>·sheh·neh <u>fpah</u>·rzheh

57

| stewed | **dušené** <u>doo</u>·sheh·neh |
| stuffed | **plněné** <u>plnyeh</u>·neh |

Special Requirements

I'm diabetic.	**Jsem diabetik.** ysehm <u>dyah</u>·beh·tihk
I'm a vegetarian.	**Jsem vegetarián.** ysehm <u>veh</u>·geh·tah·ryahn
I'm lactose intolerant.	**Mám intoleranci laktózy.** mahm ihn·toh·leh·rahn·tsih <u>lahk</u>·toh·zih
I'm allergic to...	**Mám alergii na...** mahm <u>ah</u>·lehr·gyih nah...
I can't eat...	**Nesmím jíst nic...** <u>nehs</u>·meem yeest nihts...
– dairy	– **mléčné výrobky** <u>mlehch</u>·neh <u>vee</u>·rohb·kih
– gluten	– **gluten** <u>gloo</u>·tehn
– nuts	– **ořechy** <u>orzheh</u>·khih
– pork	– **vepřové** <u>vehp</u>·rzhoh·veh
– shellfish	– **mořské plody** <u>mohrzhs</u>·keh ploh·dih
– spicy foods	– **pikantní jídla** <u>pih</u>·kahnt·nee <u>jeed</u>·lah
– wheat	– **pšeniční produkty** <u>psheh</u>·nihch·nee <u>proh</u>·dook·tih
Is it kosher?	**Je to košer?** yeh toh <u>koh</u>·shehr

Dining with Kids

Do you have children's portions?	**Máte porce pro děti?** mah·teh <u>pohr</u>·tseh proh <u>dyeh</u>·tih
A *highchair/child's seat*, please.	**Židličku/Židli pro dítě**, prosím. <u>zhihd</u>·lihch·koo/ <u>zhihd</u>·lih proh <u>dee</u>·tyeh <u>proh</u>·seem
Where can I *feed/ change* the baby?	**Kde mohu *nakojit/přebalit* dítě?** gdeh <u>moh</u>·hoo <u>nah</u>·koh·yiht/<u>przheh</u>·bah·liht <u>dee</u>·tyeh
Can you warm this?	**Můžete mi to přihřát?** <u>mooh</u>·zheh·teh mih toh <u>przhih</u>·hrzhaht

▶ For travel with children, see page 146.

Complaints

How much longer will our food be?	**Jak dlouho budeme ještě na jídlo čekat?** yahk <u>dloh</u>·hoh <u>boo</u>·deh·meh <u>yehsh</u>·tyeh nah·yeed·loh <u>cheh</u>·kaht
We can't wait any longer.	**Už nemůžeme déle čekat.** oozh <u>neh</u>·moo·zheh·meh <u>deh</u>·leh <u>cheh</u>·kaht
We're leaving.	**Odcházíme.** <u>oht</u>·khah·zee·meh
I didn't order this.	**To jsem si neobjednal♂/neobjednala♀.** toh ysehm sih <u>neh</u>·ohb·yehd·nahl♂/ <u>neh</u>·ohb·yehd·nah·lah♀
I ordered...	**Objednal♂/Objednala♀ jsem si...** <u>ohb</u>·yehd·nahl♂/<u>ohb</u>·yehd·nah·lah♀ ysehm sih...
I can't eat this.	**Nemohu to jíst.** <u>neh</u>·moh·hoo toh yeest
This is too...	**Tohle je moc...** <u>toh</u>·hleh yeh mohts...
– cold/hot	– **studené/horké** <u>stoo</u>·deh·neh/<u>hohr</u>·keh
– salty/spicy	– **slané/pikantní** <u>slah</u>·neh/<u>pih</u>·kahnt·nee
– tough/bland	– **tvrdé/mdlé** tfrdeh/mdleh
This isn't clean.	**Tohle není čisté.** <u>toh</u>·hleh <u>neh</u>·nee <u>chihs</u>·teh
This isn't fresh.	**Není to čerstvé.** <u>neh</u>·nee toh <u>chehrs</u>·tfeh

Paying

The check [bill], please.	**Účet, prosím.** <u>oo</u>·cheht <u>proh</u>·seem
We'd like to pay separately.	**Budeme platit každý samostatně.** <u>boo</u>·deh·meh <u>plah</u>·tiht <u>kazh</u>·dee <u>sah</u>·mohs·taht·nyeh
It's all together.	**Všechno dohromady.** <u>fshehkh</u>·noh <u>doh</u>·hroh·mah·dih
Is service included?	**Je v tom zahrnutá obsluha?** yeh ftohm <u>zah</u>·hrnoo·tah <u>ohp</u>·sloo·hah

What's this amount for?	**Za co je tato částka?** <u>zah</u>·tsoh yeh <u>tah</u>·toh <u>chahst</u>·kah
I didn't have that. I had...	**To jsem neměl♂/neměla♀. Měl♂/Měla♀ jsem...** toh ysehm <u>neh</u>·myehl♂/<u>neh</u>·myeh·lah♀ myehl♂/<u>myeh</u>·lah♀ ysehm...
Can I pay by credit card?	**Mohu zaplatit kreditní kartou?** moh·hoo <u>zah</u>·plah·tiht <u>kreh</u>·diht·nee kahr·toh
Can I have an *itemized bill/ a receipt*?	**Mohli byste mi *účet rozepsát/dát stvrzenku*?** moh·hlih bihs·teh mih <u>oo</u>·cheht roh·zehp·<u>saht</u>/daht stvrzehn·koo
That was a very good meal.	**Výborně jsem se najedl♂/najedla♀.** <u>vee</u>·bohr·nyeh ysehm seh <u>na</u>·yehdl♂/<u>nah</u>·yehd·lah♀

If a service charge is included in the price, you'll see **obsluha zahrnutá** (service included) on the menu in a restaurant, bar or beer hall. If the tip is not included in the bill, it's customary to leave 5–10%. Either hand the tip to your server and say **děkuji** (thank you) or **to je v pořádku** (it's OK), or simply leave the tip on the table.

Market

Where are the *carts [trolleys]/baskets*?	**Kde jsou *vozíky/košíky*?** gdeh ysoh <u>voh</u>·zee·kih/<u>koh</u>·shee·kih
Where is...?	**Kde je...?** gdeh yeh...

▶ For food items, see page 76.

I'd like some of *that/those*.	**Chtěl♂/Chtěla♀ bych *to/tamto*.** khtyehl♂/khtyeh·lah♀ bihkh toh/<u>tahm</u>·toh
Can I taste it?	**Můžu to ochutnat?** <u>moo</u>·zhoo toh <u>oh</u>·khoot·naht

I'd like...	**Chtěl**♂**/Chtěla**♀ **bych...** khtyehl♂/ khtyeh·lah♀ bihkh...
– a *kilo/half-kilo* of...	– **kilo/půl kila...** kih·loh/pool kih·lah...
– a *liter/half-liter* of...	– **litr/půl litru...** lihtr/pool liht·roo...
– a piece of...	– **kousek...** koh·sehk...
– a slice of...	– **pláteček...** plah·teh·chehk...
More/Less.	**Trošku** *vice/méně.* trohsh·koo vih·tseh/meh·nyeh
How much?	**Kolik?** koh·lihk
Where do I pay?	**Kde zaplatím?** gdeh zah·plah·teem
A bag, please.	**Tašku, prosím.** tahsh·koo proh·seem
I'm being helped.	**Už mne obsluhují.** oosh mneh ohp·sloo·hoo·yee

▶ For conversion tables, see page 175.

You May Hear...

Čím posloužím? cheem pohs·loh·zheem	Can I help you?
Co si přejete? tsoh sih przheh·yeh·teh	What would you like?
Ještě něco? yehsh·tyeh nyeh·tsoh	Anything else?
...korun. ...koh·roon	That's...crowns.

Grocery stores and supermarkets are usually open Monday to Friday from 6 a.m. to 6 p.m., while other shops from 8 a.m. to 6 p.m.; on Saturdays, stores are generally open, from 6 a.m. or 8 a.m. to noon. **Večerki** are grocery stores with longer hours of operation, generally 6 a.m. to 9 p.m., Monday–Saturday; these are sometimes open on Sunday at variable times.

KALORIE	calories
BEZ TUKU	fat free
USCHOVEJTE V CHLADU	keep refrigerated
PRODAT PŘED...	sell by...
HODIT SE PRO VEGETARIANY	suitable for vegetarians

Dishes, Utensils and Kitchen Tools

bottle opener	**otvírač na láhve** <u>oht</u>·fee·rahch <u>nah</u>·lah·hfeh
bowl	**miska** <u>mihs</u>·kah
can opener	**otvírač na plechovky** <u>oht</u>·fee·rach <u>nah</u>·pleh·khohf·kih
corkscrew	**vývrtka** <u>vee</u>·vrtkah
cup	**šálek** <u>shah</u>·lehk
fork	**vidlička** <u>vih</u>·dlihch·kah
frying pan	**pánev** <u>pah</u>·nehf
glass	**sklenice** <u>skleh</u>·nih·tseh
knife	**nůž** noozh
measuring *cup/ spoon*	**odměrka/měření lžice** <u>ohd</u>·myehr·kah/ <u>myeh</u>·rzheh·nee <u>lzhih</u>·tseh
napkin	**ubrousek** <u>oob</u>·roh·sehk
plate	**talíř** <u>tah</u>·leerzh
pot	**konvice** <u>kohn</u>·vih·tseh
saucepan	**hrnec** hrnehts
spatula	**lopatka** <u>loh</u>·paht·kah
spoon	**lžíce** <u>lzhee</u>·tseh

Meals

 Traditional Czech cuisine is rather heavy; roasted and fried meat (especially pork; another favorite is poultry), dense sauces, filling soup and stuffed dumplings are just a sampling of typical meals. Potatoes and cabbage are also staples of the Czech diet, and beer can be said to be the indispensable element of every dinner.

Breakfast

chléb khlehb	bread
džem dzhehm	jam
džus dzhoos	juice
jogurt <u>yoh</u>·goort	yogurt
káva <u>kah</u>·vah	coffee
kukuřičné vločky <u>koo</u>·koo·rzhihch·neh <u>vlohch</u>·kih	corn flakes
máslo <u>mah</u>·sloh	butter
med meht	honey
mléko <u>mleh</u>·koh	milk
topinka <u>toh</u>·pihn·kah	toast
...vejce ...<u>vehy</u>·tseh	...egg
– míchaná <u>mee</u>·khah·nah	– scrambled
– smažená <u>smah</u>·zheh·nah	– fried
– vařená <u>vah</u>·rzheh·nah	– boiled

I'd like...	**Chtěl**♂**/Chtěla**♀ **bych...** khtyehl♂/<u>khtyeh</u>·lah♀ bihkh...
More...please.	**Více...prosím.** vee·tseh...<u>proh</u>·seem
With/Without...	**S/Bez...** s/behs...
I can't have...	**Nesmím jíst nic...** <u>nehs</u>·meem yeest nihts...

63

Appetizers [Starters]

křenová rolka <u>krzheh</u>·noh·vah <u>rohl</u>·kah	ham and horseradish roll
ruská vejce <u>roos</u>·kah <u>vehy</u>·tseh	egg with mayonnaise
salám s okurkou sah·lahm <u>soh</u>·koor·koh	salami with pickles
šunka s okurkou <u>shoon</u>·kah <u>soh</u>·koor·koh	ham with pickles
šunka v aspiku <u>shoon</u>·kah <u>vahs</u>·pih·koo	ham in aspic
tlačenka s cibulí <u>tlah</u>·chehn·kah <u>stsih</u>·boo·lee	rolled pork with onion
tresčí játra s cíbulkou <u>trehs</u>·chee <u>yah</u>·trah <u>stsee</u>·bool·koh	cod liver with onion
uzený jazyk <u>oo</u>·zeh·nee <u>yah</u>·zihk	smoked tongue
zavináče <u>zah</u>·vih·nah·cheh	pickled herring [rollmops]

Soup

bramboračka <u>brahm</u>·boh·rahch·kah	a thick soup with cubed potatoes, vegetables, mushrooms and garlic
bramborová polévka <u>brahm</u>·boh·roh·vah <u>poh</u>·lehf·kah	potato soup
česneková polévka <u>chehs</u>·neh·koh·vah <u>poh</u>·lehf·kah	garlic soup
čočková polévka <u>chohch</u>·koh·vah <u>poh</u>·lehf·kah	lentil soup
fazolová polévka <u>fah</u>·zoh·loh·vah <u>poh</u>·lehf·kah	bean soup
hovězí vývar (s nudlemi) <u>hoh</u>·vyeh·zee <u>vee</u>·vahr (<u>snood</u>·leh·mih)	consommé (with noodles)

I'd like...	**Chtěl**♂/**Chtěla**♀ **bych...** khtyehl♂/<u>khtyeh</u>·lah♀ bihkh...
More...please.	**Více...prosím.** vee·tseh...<u>proh</u>·seem

hovězí vyvar s játrovými noky <u>hoh</u>·vyeh·zee <u>vee</u>·vahr <u>syah</u>·troh·vee·mih <u>noh</u>·kih	beef broth and liver dumplings
hrachová polévka s uzeným <u>hrah</u>·khoh·vah <u>poh</u>·lehf·kah <u>soo</u>·zeh·neem	pea soup with smoked meat
kuřecí vývar (se zeleninou) <u>koo</u>·rzheh·tsee <u>vee</u>·vahr (<u>seh</u>·zeh·leh·nih·noh)	chicken soup (with vegetables)
rajská polévka <u>rahy</u>·skah <u>poh</u>·lehf·kah	tomato soup
rybí polévka <u>rih</u>·bee <u>poh</u>·lehf·kah	fish soup
zeleninová polévka <u>zeh</u>·leh·nih·noh·vah <u>poh</u>·lehf·kah	vegetable soup
zelná polévka <u>zehl</u>·nah <u>poh</u>·lehf·kah	cabbage soup
zelňačka <u>zehl</u>·n'ahch·kah	a thick soup with potatoes, sauerkraut and cream

Among Czech **polévki** (soups) attention should be paid, apart from the traditional **hovězí vývar** (beef broth) with noodles, to **česnekačka** (garlic soup with egg and small pieces of toasted bread). Other popular soups are **gulášová polévka** (goulash soup) and **dršťková polévka** (tripe soup), which is generously seasoned with sweet pepper.

Fish and Seafood

candát <u>tsahn</u>·daht	pike perch
garnát <u>gahr</u>·naht	shrimp [prawn]
humr hoomr	lobster
chobotnice <u>khoh</u>·boht·nih·tseh	octopus

With/Without...	**S/Bez...** s/behs...
I can't have...	**Nesmím jíst nic...** <u>nehs</u>·meem yeest nihts...

kapr... kahpr...	carp...
– **smažený** <u>smah</u>·zheh·nee	– fried in bread crumbs
– **na černo** <u>nah</u>·chehr·noh	– in a thick sauce of vegetables, dark beer and prunes
– **na česneku** <u>nah</u>·chehs·neh·koo	– grilled with butter and garlic
kaviár <u>kah</u>·vyahr	caviar
krab krahb	crab
losos <u>loh</u>·sohs	salmon
mořský jazyk <u>mohrzh</u>·skee <u>yah</u>·zihk	sole
platýz <u>plah</u>·tees	plaice
pstruh na másle pstrooh nah <u>mah</u>·sleh	trout fried in butter
rybí filé <u>rih</u>·bee <u>fih</u>·leh	fish fillet
slaneček <u>slah</u>·neh·chehk	herring
štika <u>shtih</u>·kah	pike
treska <u>trehs</u>·kah	cod
tuňák <u>too</u>·n'ahk	tuna
ústřice <u>oo</u>·strzhih·tseh	oyster

Meat and Poultry

bažant <u>bah</u>·zhahnt	pheasant
biftek <u>bihf</u>·tehk	steak
guláš <u>goo</u>·lahsh	goulash
hovězí <u>hoh</u>·vyeh·zee	beef
husa <u>hoo</u>·sah	goose
jehněčí <u>yeh</u>·hnyeh·chee	lamb

I'd like...	**Chtěl**♂/**Chtěla**♀ **bych...** khtyehl♂/<u>khtyeh</u>·lah♀ bihkh...
More...please.	**Více...prosím.** vee·tseh...<u>proh</u>·seem

kachna <u>kahkh</u>·nah	duck
klobása <u>kloh</u>·bah·sah	sausage
králík <u>krah</u>·leek	rabbit
krůta <u>krooh</u>·tah	turkey
kuře <u>koo</u>·rzheh	chicken
párka <u>pahr</u>·kah	type of thick sausage
slanina <u>slah</u>·nih·nah	bacon
šunka <u>shoon</u>·kah	ham
telecí <u>teh</u>·leh·tsee	veal

With/Without...	**S/Bez...** s/behs...	
I can't have...	**Nesmím jíst nic...** <u>nehs</u>·meem yeest nihts...	

vepřové <u>vehp</u>·rzhoh·veh		pork
zajíc <u>zah</u>·yeets		hare
zvěřina <u>zvyeh</u>·rzhih·nah		game

rare	**krvavé** <u>krfah</u>·veh
medium	**mírně propečené** <u>meer</u>·nyeh <u>proh</u>·peh·cheh·neh
well-done	**dobře upečené** <u>dohb</u>·rzheh <u>oo</u>·peh·cheh·neh

Dumplings

bramborové knedlíky <u>brahm</u>·boh·roh·veh <u>knehd</u>·lee·kih	potato dumplings
houskové knedlíky <u>hohs</u>·koh·veh <u>knehd</u>·lee·kih	bread dumplings
švestkové knedlíky <u>shvehst</u>·koh·veh <u>knehd</u>·lee·kih	plum dumplings

i One of the best-known Czech dishes is **vepřo-knedlo-zelo** (pork with fried cabbage) and **knedlíky** (dumplings). There are two types of **knedlíky: houskové knedlíky** (made of flour) and **bramborové knedlíky** (made with potatoes). The latter are usually served with duck or goose together with red cabbage boiled in red wine. The highlight of Czech cuisine is **svíčková na smetaně** (beef fillet in cream and vegetable sauce of a slightly sour taste), served naturally with **knedlíky**.

Vegetables

brambor <u>brahm</u>·bohr	potato
celer <u>tseh</u>·lehr	celery
cibule <u>tsih</u>·boo·leh	onion

I'd like...	**Chtěl**♂/**Chtěla**♀ **bych...** khtyehl♂/<u>khtyeh</u>·lah♀ bihkh...
More...please.	**Více...prosím.** vee·tseh...<u>proh</u>·seem

68

cuketa <u>tsoo</u>·keh·tah		zucchini [courgette]
červená řepa <u>chehr</u>·veh·nah <u>rzheh</u>·pah		beet [beetroot]
česnek <u>chehs</u>·nehk		garlic
fazolové lusky <u>fah</u>·zoh·loh·veh <u>loos</u>·kih		green beans
houba <u>hoh</u>·bah		mushroom
hrášek <u>hrah</u>·shehk		peas
jarní cibulka <u>yahr</u>·nee <u>tsih</u>·bool·kah		spring onion
květák <u>kvyeh</u>·tahk		cauliflower
lilek <u>lih</u>·lehk		eggplant [aubergine]
mrkev mrkehf		carrot
okurka <u>oh</u>·koor·kah		cucumber
paprika <u>pahp</u>·rih·kah		pepper
pórek <u>poh</u>·rehk		leek
rajče <u>rahy</u>·cheh		tomato
salát <u>sah</u>·laht		lettuce
šalotka <u>shah</u>·loht·kah		shallot
zelí <u>zeh</u>·lee		cabbage
žampiony <u>zhahm</u>·pyoh·nih		mushrooms

Spices and Staples

chléb khlehb	bread
cukr tsookr	sugar
mouka <u>moh</u>·kah	flour
máslo <u>mah</u>·sloh	butter
ořech <u>oh</u>·rzhekh	nut

With/Without...	**S/Bez...** s/behs...
I can't have...	**Nesmím jíst nic...** nehs·meem yeest nihts...

ocet <u>oh</u>·tseht	vinegar
olej <u>oh</u>·lehy	oil
pepř pehprzh	pepper (seasoning)
rýže <u>ree</u>·zheh	rice
sůl sool	salt
těstoviny <u>tyehs</u>·toh·vih·nih	pasta

Fruit

banán <u>bah</u>·nahn	banana
borůvka <u>boh</u>·roof·kah	blueberry
broskev <u>brohs</u>·kehv	peach
grep grehp	grapefruit
hrozno <u>hrohz</u>·noh	grape
jablko <u>yah</u>·blkoh	apple
jahoda <u>yah</u>·hoh·dah	strawberry
malina <u>mah</u>·lih·nah	raspberry
meloun <u>meh</u>·lohn	melon
meruňka <u>meh</u>·roon'·kah	apricot
pomeranč <u>poh</u>·meh·rahnch	orange
švestka <u>shfehst</u>·kah	plum
třešeň <u>trzheh</u>·shehn'	cherry
višeň <u>vih</u>·shehn'	sour cherry
vodní meloun <u>vohd</u>·nee <u>meh</u>·lohn	watermelon

Cheese

jemný sýr <u>yehm</u>·nee seer	mild cheese

I'd like...	**Chtěl**♂/**Chtěla**♀ **bych...** khtyehl♂/<u>khtyeh</u>·lah♀ bihkh...
More...please.	**Více...prosím.** vee·tseh...<u>proh</u>·seem

kozí sýr <u>koh</u>·zee seer	goat cheese
měkký tvaroh <u>myehk</u>·kee <u>tfah</u>·rohh	cottage cheese
Niva® <u>nih</u>·vah	common brand of blue cheese available
ostrý sýr <u>ohs</u>·tree seer	pungent cheese
ovčí sýr <u>ohf</u>·chee seer	ewe's milk cheese
plísňový sýr <u>plees</u>·n'oh·vee seer	blue cheese
smažený sýr <u>sma</u>·zhe·nee seer	cheese fried in bread crumbs
smetanový sýr <u>smeh</u>·tah·noh·vee seer	cream cheese
syrečky <u>sih</u>·rehch·kih	pungent cheese made with beer
tvrdý sýr tfrdee seer	hard cheese

Dessert

jablečný závin <u>yahb</u>·lehch·nee <u>zah</u>·vihn	apple strudel
kobliha <u>kohb</u>·lih·hah	donut
lívance <u>lee</u>·vahn·tseh	small pancakes, spread with plums and a layer of cottage cheese, topped with yogurt or thick sour cream
makový koláč <u>mah</u>·koh·vee <u>koh</u>·lahch	poppy seed cake
medovník <u>meh</u>·dohv·neek	honey cake
ovocný koláč <u>oh</u>·vohts·nee <u>koh</u>·lahch	fruit cake

With/Without...	**S/Bez...** s/behs...
I can't have...	**Nesmím jíst nic...** <u>nehs</u>·meem yeest nihts...

ovocný koláč s drobenkou <u>oh</u>·vohts·nee koh·lahch <u>sdroh</u>·behn·koh	fruit crumble pie
palačinka <u>pah</u>·lah·chihn·kah	thin pancake
švestkové knedlíky <u>shvehst</u>·koh·veh knehd·lee·kih	plum dumplings sprinkled with curd cheese and sugar and covered with melted butter
trubičky se šlehačkou <u>troo</u>·bihch·kih seh·shleh·hahch·koh	brandy cake rolls with cream
tvarohové taštičky <u>tfah</u>·roh·hoh·veh tash·tihch·kih	cottage cheese pastries
zmrzlina <u>zmrzlih</u>·nah	ice cream

Drinks

Essential

May I see the *wine list/drink menu*, please?	**Smím prosit *vínný lístek/nápojový lístek*?** smeem <u>proh</u>·siht <u>veen</u>·nee lees·tehk/ <u>nah</u>·poh·yoh·vee lees·tehk
What do you recommend?	**Co mi můžete doporoučit?** tsoh mih <u>moo</u>·zheh·teh <u>doh</u>·poh·roh·chiht
I'd like a *bottle/ glass* of *red/white* wine.	**Chtěl♂/Chtěla♀ bych *láhev/pohár* *červeného/bílého* vína.** khtyehl♂/<u>khteh</u>·lah♀ bihkh <u>lah</u>·hef/<u>poh</u>·hahr <u>chehr</u>·veh·neh·hoh/ <u>bee</u>·leh·hoh <u>vee</u>·nah
The house wine, please.	**Stolní víno, prosím.** <u>stohl</u>·nee <u>vee</u>·noh <u>proh</u>·seem

Another *bottle/ glass*, please.	**Ještě jednu *láhev/pohár*, prosím.** <u>yeh</u>·shtyeh yehd·noo <u>lah</u>·hehf/<u>poh</u>·hahr proh·seem
I'd like a local beer.	**Chtěl♂/Chtěla♀ bych místní pivo.** khtyehl♂/ khtyeh·lah♀ bihkh <u>meest</u>·nee pih·voh
Can I buy you a drink?	**Mohu vám objednat něco k pití?** moh·hoo vahm <u>ohb</u>·yehd·naht <u>nyeh</u>·tsoh <u>kpih</u>·tee
Cheers!	**Na zdraví!** <u>nah</u>·zdrah·vee
A *coffee/tea*, please.	**Kávu/Čaj, prosím.** <u>kah</u>·voo/chahy <u>proh</u>·seem
..., please.	**...prosím.** ...<u>proh</u>·seem
– Juice	**– Džus** dzhoos
– Soda	**– Sodou** <u>soh</u>·doh
– (*Sparkling/Still*) Water	**– Vodu (*s bublinkami/bez bublinek*)** <u>voh</u>·doo (<u>zboob</u>·lihn·kah·mih/<u>behz</u>·boob·lih·nehk)
Is the tap water safe to drink?	**Může se pít kohoutková voda?** <u>moo</u>·zheh seh peet <u>koh</u>·hoht·koh·vah <u>voh</u>·dah

Non-alcoholic Drinks

čaj chahy	tea
...džus ...dzhoos	...juice
– jablečný <u>yahb</u>·lehch·nee	– apple
– pomerančový poh·meh·rahn·choh·vee	– orange
– rajský <u>rahy</u>·skee	– tomato
horkou čokoládu <u>hohr</u>·koh choh·koh·<u>lah</u>·doo	hot chocolate
(*bílou/černou*) kávu (<u>bee</u>·loh/<u>chehr</u>·noh) <u>kah</u>·voo	coffee (*with milk/ black*)
kávu s *cukrem/umělým sladidlem* <u>kah</u>·voo s <u>tsook</u>·rehm/<u>oo</u>·myeh·leem <u>slah</u>·dih·dlehm	coffee with *sugar/ artificial sweetener*
kávu bez kofeinu <u>kah</u>·voo <u>behs</u>·koh·feh·yih·noo	decaffeinated coffee
kolu <u>koh</u>·loo	cola

limonádu <u>lih</u>·moh·nah·doo	lemonade
mléko <u>mleh</u>·koh	milk
mléčný koktejl <u>mleh</u>·chnee <u>kohk</u>·tehyl	milk shake
minerálku (s bublinkami / bez bublinek) <u>mih</u>·neh·rahl·koo (<u>zboob</u>·lihn·kah·mih / behz·boob·lih·nehk)	*(sparkling / still)* mineral water

i Among hot drinks, the most popular is **káva** (coffee), enjoyed not only as a breakfast beverage, but also before and after noon, in the evening and at night. Prague is home to many popular **kavárny** (coffee houses); these are excellent places to enjoy local life. As to **čaj** (tea), Czechs themselves joke that it is a beverage for kids, while adults drink it only in winter (and then with rum). Among cold drinks, a typically Czech beverage is **Kofola®** (a cola that includes fruit extracts), which can be bought not only in bottles or cans, but also from the barrel as **čepovaná kofola**. Mineral water is also readily available; well-known brands include: **Aquila®**, **Dobrá Voda®**, **Hanácka Kyselka®**, **Karlovarské®**, **Poděbradka®**, **Rajec®** and **Toma Voda®**.

You May Hear...

Mohu vám objednat něco k pití? <u>moh</u>·hoo vahm <u>ohb</u>·yehd·naht <u>nyeh</u>·tsoh <u>kpih</u>·tee | Can I get you a drink?

Bílou/S cukrem? <u>bee</u>·loh/<u>stsook</u>·rehm | With *milk/sugar*?

Voda s bublinkami nebo bez bublinek? <u>voh</u>·dah <u>zboob</u>·lihn·kah·mih <u>neh</u>·boh <u>behz</u>·boob·lih·nehk | Sparkling or still water?

Aperitifs, Cocktails and Liqueurs

anýzovka <u>ah</u>·nee·zohf·kah	aniseed liqueur
brandy <u>brehn</u>·dih	brandy
džin dzhihn	gin
džin fiz dzhihn fihz	gin fizz
džin s tonikem dzhihn <u>stoh</u>·nih·kehm	gin and tonic
meruňkovice <u>meh</u>·roon'·koh·vih·tseh	apricot brandy
pálenka <u>pah</u>·lehn·kah	brandy
slivovice <u>slih</u>·voh·vih·tseh	plum brandy
šery <u>sheh</u>·rih	sherry
vodka <u>voht</u>·kah	vodka
vermut <u>vehr</u>·moot	vermouth
whisky <u>vihs</u>·kih	whisky

Beer

černé <u>chehr</u>·neh	stout
láhvové <u>lah</u>·hfoh·veh	bottled
ležák <u>leh</u>·zhahk	lager
místní pivo <u>meest</u>·nee <u>pih</u>·voh	local beer
pivo <u>pih</u>·voh	beer
plzeňské <u>plzehn'</u>·skeh	pilsner

pšeničné pivo <u>psheh</u>·nih·chn**eh** <u>pih</u>·voh	wheat beer
světlé <u>svyeht</u>·leh	light
točené <u>toh</u>·cheh·neh	draft [draught]

---

i The turning point for Czech brewing was October 5, 1842, when the technology of bottom fermentation was used for the first time and **světlý ležák** (pale lager) **Pilsner Urquell®** was produced. Apart from **Pilsner Urquell®** (called simply **Plzeň** by Czechs), other popular Czech beer brands are: **Budějovický Budvar®**, **Velkopopovický Kozel®**, **Radegast®**, **Staropramen®** and **Gambrinus®**. In addition to these, one may also order **řezane**: dark and light beer poured into one glass in such a way that it creates two distinct layers.

Wine

...víno ...<u>vee</u>·noh	...wine
– **bílé** <u>bee</u>·leh	– white
– **červené** <u>chehr</u>·veh·neh	– red
– **růžové** <u>roo</u>·zhoh·veh	– blush [rosé]
– **sladké** <u>slaht</u>·keh	– sweet
– **suché** <u>soo</u>·kheh	– dry
– **šumivé** <u>shoo</u>·mih·veh	– sparkling

Menu Reader

alkoholický nápoj <u>ahl</u>·koh·hoh·lihts·kee <u>nah</u>·pohy	alcoholic drink
ananas <u>ah</u>·nah·nahs	pineapple
angrešt <u>ahn</u>·gresht	gooseberry
anýz <u>ah</u>·neez	aniseed

anýzovka <u>ah</u>·nee·zohf·kah	aniseed liqueur
aperitiv <u>ah</u>·peh·rih·tihf	aperitif
arašíd <u>ah</u>·rah·sheed	peanut
artyčok <u>ahr</u>·tih·chohk	artichoke
aspik <u>ahs</u>·pihk	jelly
avokádo <u>ah</u>·voh·kah·doh	avocado
banán <u>bah</u>·nahn	banana
banán v čokoládí <u>bah</u>·nahn <u>fchoh</u>·koh·lah·dee	chocolate-covered banana
bazalka <u>bah</u>·zahl·kah	basil
bažant <u>bah</u>·zhahnt	pheasant
bez kofeinu <u>behs</u>·koh·feh·yih·noo	decaffeinated
biftek <u>bihf</u>·tehk	steak
bílé hrozen <u>bee</u>·leh <u>hroh</u>·zehn	green grape
bílé zelí <u>bee</u>·leh <u>zeh</u>·lee	white cabbage
bílek <u>bee</u>·lehk	egg white
bílý chléb <u>bee</u>·lee khlehb	white bread
bob bohb	broad bean
bobkový list <u>bohb</u>·koh·vee lihst	bay leaf
bonbón <u>bohn</u>·bohn	candy [sweet]
borůvka <u>boh</u>·roof·kah	blueberry
borůvkový knedlík <u>boh</u>·roof·koh·vee <u>knehd</u>·leek	blueberry dumpling
borůvkový koláč <u>boh</u>·roof·koh·vee <u>koh</u>·lahch	blueberry pie
brambor <u>brahm</u>·bohr	potato
bramboračka <u>brahm</u>·boh·rahch·kah	thick soup with potatoes and vegetables
bramborák <u>brahm</u>·boh·rahk	potato pancake
bramborová kaše <u>brahm</u>·boh·roh·vah <u>kah</u>·sheh	mashed potato

bramborová polévka <u>brahm</u>·boh·roh·vah <u>poh</u>·lehf·kah	potato soup
bramborové hranolky <u>brahm</u>·boh·roh·veh <u>hrah</u>·nohl·kih	French fries
bramborové taštičky s masitou nádivkou <u>brahm</u>·boh·roh·veh <u>tahsh</u>·tihch·kih <u>smah</u>·sih·toh <u>nah</u>·dihf·koh	potato ravioli with meat filling
bramborový knedlík <u>brahm</u>·boh·roh·vee <u>knehd</u>·leek	potato dumpling
bramborový kroket <u>brahm</u>·boh·roh·vee <u>kroh</u>·keht	potato croquette
brokolice <u>broh</u>·koh·lih·tseh	broccoli
broskev <u>brohs</u>·kehf	peach
brusinka <u>broo</u>·sihn·kah	cranberry
bůček <u>boo</u>·chehk	brisket

buchta <u>boo</u>·khtah	sweet bun
burský oříšek <u>boor</u>·skee <u>oh</u>·rzhee·shehk	peanut
bylinka <u>bih</u>·lihn·kah	herb
bylinková směs <u>bih</u>·lihn·koh·vah smyehs	mixed herbs
candát <u>tsahn</u>·daht	pike perch
celer <u>tseh</u>·lehr	celery
celozrnná mouka <u>tseh</u>·lohz·rnah <u>moh</u>·kah	whole-wheat flour
cemr tsehmr	loin
cibule <u>tsih</u>·boo·leh	onion
citrón <u>tsih</u>·trohn	lemon
citrónový džus <u>tsiht</u>·roh·noh·vee dzhoos	lemon juice
cuketa <u>tsoo</u>·keh·tah	zucchini [courgette]
cukr tsookr	sugar
cukrová kukuřice <u>tsook</u>·roh·vah <u>koo</u>·koo·rzhih·tseh	corn [sweet corn]
cukroví <u>tsook</u>·roh·vee	small sweet pastries
čaj chahy	tea
čekanka <u>cheh</u>·kahn·kah	chicory
černou <u>chehr</u>·noh	black (coffee)
černý rybíz <u>chehr</u>·nee <u>rih</u>·bees	black currant
čerstvý <u>chehrs</u>·tfee	fresh
čerstvý ovoc <u>chehrs</u>·tfee <u>oh</u>·vohts	fresh fruit
čerstvý tvaroh <u>chehrs</u>·tfee <u>tfah</u>·roh	fresh curd cheese
červená řepa <u>chehr</u>·veh·nah <u>rzheh</u>·pah	beet [beetroot]
červené zelí <u>chehr</u>·veh·neh zeh·lee	red cabbage
červený <u>chehr</u>·veh·nee	red (wine)
červený hrozen <u>chehr</u>·veh·nee <u>hroh</u>·zehn	red grape
červený rybíz <u>chehr</u>·veh·nee <u>rih</u>·bees	red currant

česnek <u>chehs</u>·nehk	garlic
česneková majonéza <u>chehs</u>·neh·koh·vah <u>mah</u>·yoh·neh·zah	garlic mayonnaise
česneková omáčka <u>chehs</u>·neh·koh·vah <u>oh</u>·mah·chkah	garlic sauce
česneková polévka <u>chehs</u>·neh·koh·vah poh·lehf·kah	garlic soup
čevapčiči <u>cheh</u>·vahp·chih·chih	meatballs
čínské zelí <u>cheen</u>·skeh <u>zeh</u>·lee	Chinese cabbage
čistý <u>chihs</u>·tee	straight [neat]
čočka <u>chohch</u>·kah	lentil
čočková polévka <u>chohch</u>·koh·vah <u>poh</u>·lehf·kah	lentil soup
čočkový salát <u>chohch</u>·koh·vee <u>sah</u>·laht	lentil salad
čokoláda <u>choh</u>·koh·lah·dah	chocolate
chlazený <u>khlah</u>·zeh·nee	chilled, iced (drink)
chlazený nápoj <u>khlah</u>·zeh·nee <u>nah</u>·pohy	cold drink
chléb khlehb	bread
chlebíček <u>khleh</u>·bee·chehk	open sandwich
chlupatý knedlík <u>khloo</u>·pah·tee <u>knehd</u>·leek	dumpling with diced, smoked meat and sauerkraut
chobotnice <u>khoh</u>·boht·nih·tseh	octopus
chřest khrzhehst	asparagus
chuťovky <u>khoo</u>·t'ohf·kih	spicy appetizers [starters]
datle <u>daht</u>·leh	date
dezert <u>deh</u>·zehrt	dessert
dezertní víno <u>deh</u>·zehrt·nee <u>vee</u>·noh	dessert wine
divočák <u>dih</u>·voh·chahk	wild boar

domácí doh·mah·tsee	homemade
dort dohrt	cake
dršťková polévka drsht'koh·vah poh·lehf·kah	tripe soup
dršťky drsht'kih	tripe
drůbež droo·behzh	poultry
drůbky droob·kih	giblets
dušená ryba doo·sheh·nah rih·bah	steamed fish
dušená rýže doo·sheh·nah ree·zheh	steamed rice
dušené ovoce doo·sheh·neh oh·voh·tseh	stewed fruit
dušené telecí maso na víně doo·sheh·neh teh·leh·tsee mah·soh nah·vee·nyeh	veal braised in wine
dýně dee·nyeh	pumpkin
džem dzhehm	jam
džin dzhihn	gin
džin s tonikem dzhihn stoh·nih·kehm	gin and tonic
džus dzhoos	juice
estragon ehs·trah·gohn	tarragon
fazole fah·zoh·leh	beans
fazolová polévka fah·zoh·loh·vah poh·lehf·kah	bean soup
fazolové klíčky fah·zoh·loh·veh kleech·kih	bean sprouts
fenykl feh·nihkl	fennel
fík feek	fig
francouzská zálivka frahn·tsohs·kah zah·lihf·kah	vinaigrette [French dressing]
granát grah·naht	shrimp [prawn]
granátové jablko grah·nah·toh·veh yahbl·koh	pomegranate
gratinovaný grah·tih·noh·vah·nee	au gratin
grep grehp	grapefruit

gril grihl	grill
grilované kuře grih·loh·vah·neh koo·rzheh	grilled chicken
grilovaný na dřevěném uhlí grih·loh·vah·nee nah·drzheh·vyeh·nehm oo·hlee	charcoal-grilled
guláš goo·lahsh	goulash (stew)
gulášová polévka goo·lah·shoh·vah poh·lehf·kah	goulash soup
heřmánkový čaj hehrzh·mahn·koh·vee chahy	chamomile tea
hlavní jídla hlahv·nee yeed·lah	entrées
hodně kořeněný hohd·nyeh koh·rzheh·nyeh·nee	highly seasoned
holoub hoh·lohb	pigeon
horká voda hohr·kah voh·dah	hot water
horkou čokoládu hohr·koh choh·koh·lah·doo	hot chocolate
horký hohr·kee	hot (temperature)
hořčice hohrzh·chih·tseh	mustard
houba hoh·bah	mushroom
houska hohs·kah	roll
houskový knedlík hohs·koh·vee knehd·leek	bread dumpling
hovězí hoh·vyeh·zee	beef
hovězí pečeně hoh·vyeh·zee peh·cheh·nyeh	roast beef
hovězí tokáň hoh·vyeh·zee toh·kahn'	beef in wine and tomato purée
hovězí vývar hoh·vyeh·zee vee·vahr	beef broth
hovězí vývar s játrovými knedlíčky hoh·vyeh·zee vee·vahr syah·troh·vee·mih knehd·leech·kih	beef broth with liver dumplings
hrachor hrah·khohr	sweet peas [mangetout]

hrachová polévka s uzeným masem hrah·khoh·vah poh·lehf·kah soo·zeh·neem mah·sehm	pea soup with smoked meat
hranolky hrah·nohl·kih	French fries
hrášek hrah·shehk	peas
hrozinka hroh·zihn·kah	raisin
hruška hruh·shkah	pear
hřebíček hrzheh·bee·chehk	clove
humr hoomr	lobster
husa hoo·sah	goose
jablečný džus yahb·lehch·nee dzhoos	apple juice
jablečný závin yahb·lehch·nee zah·vihn	apple strudel
jablko yahbl·koh	apple
jablkový koláč yahbl·koh·vee koh·lahch	apple pie
jahoda yah·hoh·dah	strawberry
jarní cibulka yahr·nee tsih·bool·kah	spring onion
játra yah·trah	liver
játrová paštika yah·troh·vah pahsh·tih·kah	liver paté
játrové knedlíčky yah·troh·veh kneh·dleech·kih	liver balls (served in broth)
jazyk yah·zihk	tongue
jehněčí yeh·hnyeh·chee	lamb
jehněčí guláš yeh·hnyeh·chee goo·lahsh	lamb stew
jehněčí kýta yeh·hnyeh·chee kee·tah	leg of lamb
jelení yeh·leh·nee	venison
jelínek yeh·lee·nehk	brandy
jelito yeh·lih·toh	black pudding
jemný yehm·nee	mild (flavor)
jídelní lístek yee·dehl·nee lees·tehk	menu

jídlo <u>yeed</u>·loh	dish (meal)
jitrnice <u>yiht</u>·rnih·tseh	white sausage
jogurt <u>yoh</u>·goort	yogurt
kachna <u>kahkh</u>·nah	duck
kakao <u>kah</u>·kah·oh	cocoa
kandované ovoce <u>kahn</u>·doh·vah·neh <u>oh</u>·voh·tseh	candied fruit
kapar <u>kah</u>·pahr	caper
kapoun <u>kah</u>·pohn	capon
kapr kahpr	carp
kapr na černo kahpr <u>nah</u>·chehr·noh	baked carp in beer, prune and vegetable sauce
kapr na česneku kahpr <u>nah</u>·chehs·neh·koo	carp grilled with butter and garlic
kapr na kmíně kapr <u>nah</u>·kmee·nyeh	carp baked with caraway seeds
kapustová polévka <u>kah</u>·poos·toh·vah <u>poh</u>·lehf·kah	cabbage soup
karafa <u>kah</u>·rah·fah	carafe
karamel <u>kah</u>·rah·mehl	caramel
Karlovarská Becherovka® <u>kahr</u>·loh·vahrs·kah <u>beh</u>·kheh·rohf·kah	bitter herb liqueur
kaštan <u>kah</u>·shtahn	chestnut
káva <u>kah</u>·vah	coffee
kaviár <u>kah</u>·vyahr	caviar
kečup <u>keh</u>·choop	ketchup
kiwi <u>kee</u>·vee	kiwi fruit
klobáska <u>kloh</u>·bahs·kah	sausage made with coarsely ground pork
kmín kmeen	caraway

knedlík <u>knehd</u>·leek	dumpling
knedlík s vejci <u>knehd</u>·leek <u>sfehy</u>·tsih	dumpling with scrambled eggs
kobliha <u>kohb</u>·lih·hah	donut
kokos <u>koh</u>·kohs	coconut
koláč <u>koh</u>·lahch	pie (sweet or savory)
koláček <u>koh</u>·lah·chehk	tartlette (sweet or savory)
kompot <u>kohm</u>·poht	stewed fruit
konsomé <u>kohn</u>·soh·meh	consommé
kopr kohpr	dill
koroptev <u>koh</u>·rohp·tehf	partridge
kořeněný <u>koh</u>·rzheh·nyeh·nee	hot, spicy, seasoned
koření <u>koh</u>·rzheh·nee	seasoning, spices
kost kohst	bone
kotleta <u>koht</u>·leh·tah	chop
koza <u>koh</u>·zah	goat
kozí sýr <u>koh</u>·zee seer	goat cheese
krab krahb	crab
krájený <u>krah</u>·yeh·nee	sliced
králík <u>krah</u>·leek	rabbit
králík na smetaně <u>krah</u>·leek <u>nah</u>·smeh·tah·nyeh	roast rabbit in rich cream sauce
krekry <u>krehk</u>·rih	crackers
krémovitá polévka <u>kreh</u>·moh·vih·tah <u>poh</u>·lehf·kah	cream soup
kroketa <u>kroh</u>·keh·tah	croquette
kroupy <u>kroh</u>·pih	barley

krůta <u>kroo</u>·tah	turkey
křen krzhehn	horseradish
křepelka <u>krzheh</u>·pehl·kah	quail
kukuřice <u>koo</u>·koo·rzhih·tseh	corn
kuře <u>kooh</u>·rzheh	chicken
kuře na paprice <u>koo</u>·rzheh <u>nah</u>·pahp·rih·tseh	pan-roasted chicken with creamy paprika sauce
kuře pečené s nádivkou <u>koo</u>·rzheh peh·cheh·neh <u>snah</u>·dihf·koh	roast chicken with stuffing
kuřecí játra <u>koo</u>·rzheh·tsee yaht·rah	chicken liver
kuřecí prso <u>koo</u>·rzheh·tsee prsoh	breast of chicken
kuřecí vývar <u>koo</u>·rzheh·tsee <u>vee</u>·vahr	chicken broth
květák <u>kfyeh</u>·tahk	cauliflower
kyselé okurky <u>kih</u>·seh·leh <u>oh</u>·koor·kih	sour pickles
kyselé zelí <u>kih</u>·seh·leh <u>zeh</u>·lee	sauerkraut
kýta <u>kee</u>·tah	leg (cut of meat)
langoš <u>lahn</u>·gohsh	fried dough coated in garlic
led lehd	ice
ledvinky <u>lehd</u>·vihn·kih	kidneys
lehký <u>lehh</u>·kee	light (sauce, etc.)
ležák <u>leh</u>·zhahk	lager
lihovina <u>lih</u>·hoh·vih·nah	spirits
likér <u>lih</u>·kehr	liqueur
lilek <u>lih</u>·lehk	eggplant [aubergine]
limetta <u>lih</u>·meht·tah	lime
limettový džus <u>lih</u>·meht·toh·vee dzhoos	lime juice
limonáda <u>lih</u>·moh·nah·dah	lemonade

lískový ořech lees·koh·vee <u>oh</u>·rzhehkh	hazelnut
lístkové těsto <u>leest</u>·koh·veh <u>tyehs</u>·toh	puff pastry
lišky <u>lihsh</u>·kih	chanterelle mushrooms
lívance <u>lee</u>·vahn·tseh	small pancakes with plum and cottage cheese, topped with yogurt or sour cream
lívanečky <u>lee</u>·vah·nehch·kih	fritters
losos <u>loh</u>·sohs	salmon
majonéza <u>mahy</u>·neh·zah	mayonnaise
majoránka <u>mah</u>·yoh·rahn·kah	marjoram
mák mahk	poppy seeds
makový koláč <u>mah</u>·koh·vee <u>koh</u>·lahch	poppy seed cake
makrela <u>mahk</u>·reh·lah	mackerel
malé občerstvení <u>mah</u>·leh <u>ohb</u>·chehr·stfeh·nee	snacks
malina <u>mah</u>·lih·nah	raspberry
mandarínka <u>mahn</u>·dah·reen·kah	tangerine
mandle <u>mahn</u>·dleh	almond
marcipán <u>mahr</u>·tsih·pahn	marzipan
marinovaný (v octě) <u>mah</u>·rih·noh·vah·nee (<u>fots</u>·tyeh)	marinated (in vinegar)
marmeládu <u>mahr</u>·meh·lah·doo	jam
máslo <u>mahs</u>·loh	butter
maso <u>mah</u>·soh	meat
masová směs na roštu <u>mah</u>·soh·vah smyehs <u>nah</u>·rohsh·too	mixed grill
masový a zeleninový vývar <u>mah</u>·soh·vee ah <u>zeh</u>·leh·nih·noh·vee <u>vee</u>·vahr	meat and vegetable broth

máta <u>mah</u>·tah	mint
mečoun <u>meh</u>·chohn	swordfish
med meht	honey
medovnik <u>meh</u>·doh·vnih	honey cake
melasa <u>meh</u>·lah·sah	molasses [treacle]
meloun <u>meh</u>·lohn	melon
meruňka <u>meh</u>·roon'·kah	apricot
meruňkovice <u>meh</u>·roon'·koh·vih·tseh	apricot brandy
meruňkový knedlík <u>meh</u>·roon'·koh·vee knehd·leek	apricot dumpling
míchaná zelenina <u>mee</u>·khah·nah zeh·leh·nih·nah	mixed vegetables
míchaný salát <u>mee</u>·khah·nee sah·laht	mixed salad
minerálka/minerální voda <u>mih</u>·neh·rahl·kah/ <u>mih</u>·neh·rahl·nih <u>voh</u>·dah	mineral water
místní speciality <u>mees</u>·tnee <u>speh</u>·tsyah·lih·tih	local specialties
mléčný koktejl <u>mlehch</u>·nee <u>kohk</u>·tehyl	milk shake
mléko <u>mleh</u>·koh	milk
mleté maso <u>mleh</u>·teh <u>mah</u>·soh	ground meat [mince]
moravský vrabec <u>moh</u>·rahfs·kee <u>vrah</u>·behts	stewed slice of pork stuffed with ham, egg and pickle
moruše <u>moh</u>·roo·sheh	mulberry
mořský jazyk <u>mohrzh</u>·skee <u>yah</u>·zihk	sole
moučník <u>mohch</u>·neek	dessert
mouka <u>moh</u>·kah	flour
mozeček <u>moh</u>·zeh·chehk	brains
mrkev mrkehf	carrot

muškátový oříšek <u>moosh</u>·kah·toh·vee <u>oh</u>·rzhee·shehk	nutmeg
na česneku <u>nah</u>·chehs·neh·koo	in garlic
na grilu <u>nah</u>·grih·loo	grilled
na kosti <u>nah</u>·kohs·tih	on the bone
na másle <u>nah</u>·mah·sleh	sautéed
na oleji <u>nah</u>·oh·leh·yih	in oil
na roštu <u>nah</u>·rohsh·too	barbecued
na rožni <u>nah</u>·rohzh·nih	spit-roasted
na špízu <u>nah</u>·shpee·zoo	skewered
nadívané olivy <u>nah</u>·dee·vah·neh <u>oh</u>·lih·vih	stuffed olives
nádivka <u>nah</u>·dihf·kah	stuffing
nakládaná okurka <u>nah</u>·klah·dah·nah <u>oh</u>·koor·kah	pickle
nakládané houby <u>nah</u>·klah·dah·neh <u>hoh</u>·bih	pickled mushrooms
nakládaný <u>nah</u>·klah·dah·nee	marinated
nakrájený na plátky <u>nah</u>·krah·yeh·nee <u>nah</u>·plaht·kih	sliced
nakyselo <u>nah</u>·kih·seh·loh	sour (taste)
naměkko <u>nah</u>·myehk·koh	soft-boiled (eggs)
nápojový lístek <u>nah</u>·poh·yoh·vee <u>lees</u>·tehk	wine list
naťový celer <u>nah</u>·ťoh·vee <u>tseh</u>·lehr	celery
natvrdo <u>nah</u>·tfrdoh	hard-boiled (eggs)
nealkoholické nápoje <u>neh</u>·ahl·koh·hoh·lihts·keh <u>nah</u>·poh·yeh	non-alcoholic drinks
nektarinka <u>nehk</u>·tah·rihn·kah	nectarine
Niva® <u>nih</u>·vah	brand of blue cheese
nudle <u>nood</u>·leh	noodles

nudle s mákem <u>nood</u>·leh <u>smah</u>·kehm	wide noodles with poppy seeds, butter and sugar
nugát <u>noo</u>·gaht	nougat
obalovaný (ve strouhance) <u>oh</u>·bah·loh·vah·**nee** (<u>veh</u>·stroh·hahn·tseh)	breaded
oběd <u>oh</u>·byeht	lunch
obloha <u>ohb</u>·loh·hah	garnish
obložený chlebíček <u>ohb</u>·loh·zheh·nee <u>khleh</u>·bee·chehk	open sandwich
okoun <u>oh</u>·kohn	perch
okurka <u>oh</u>·koor·kah	cucumber
oliva <u>oh</u>·lih·vah	olive
omáčka <u>oh</u>·mahch·kah	gravy, sauce
omeleta <u>oh</u>·meh·leh·tah	omelet
oplatek <u>ohp</u>·lah·tehk	wafer
ořech <u>oh</u>·rzhehkh	nut
ostružina <u>ohs</u>·troo·zhih·nah	blackberry
ostružinová marmeláda <u>ohs</u>·troo·zhih·noh·vah <u>mahr</u>·meh·**lah**·dah	blackberry jam
ostružinový koláč <u>ohs</u>·troo·zhih·noh·vee <u>koh</u>·lahch	blackberry pie
ostrý <u>ohst</u>·ree	hot (spicy)
ovesná kaše <u>oh</u>·vehs·nah <u>kah</u>·sheh	oatmeal [porridge]
ovoc <u>oh</u>·vohts	fruit
ovoce z konzervy <u>oh</u>·voh·tseh <u>skohn</u>·zehr·vih	canned fruit
ovocný džus <u>oh</u>·vohts·nee dzhoos	fruit juice
ovocný koláč <u>oh</u>·vohts·nee <u>koh</u>·lahch	fruit pie
ovocný kompot <u>oh</u>·vohts·nee <u>kohm</u>·poht	fruit compote

ovocný nápoj <u>oh</u>·vohts·nee <u>nah</u>·pohy	fruit drink
palačinka <u>pah</u>·lah·chihn·kah	thin pancake
palačinka s čokoládou <u>pah</u>·lah·chihn·kah <u>schoh</u>·koh·lah·doh	thin pancake with chocolate sauce
palačinka s ovocem a se zmrzlinou <u>pah</u>·lah·chihn·kah <u>soh</u>·voh·tsehm ah <u>seh</u>·zmrzlih·noh	thin pancake with fruit and ice cream
pálenka <u>pah</u>·lehn·kah	brandy
párek <u>pah</u>·rehk	thin sausage, made with finely ground pork
párek v rohlíku <u>pah</u>·rehk <u>vroh</u>·hlee·koo	hot dog
paštika <u>pahsh</u>·tih·kah	pâté
pažitka <u>pah</u>·zhiht·kah	chives
pečená kachna <u>peh</u>·cheh·nah <u>kahkh</u>·nah	roast duck
pečená ryba <u>peh</u>·cheh·nah <u>rih</u>·bah	baked fish
pečeně <u>peh</u>·cheh·nyeh	roast
pečené kuře <u>peh</u>·cheh·neh <u>koo</u>·rzheh	roast chicken
pečeně se slaninou <u>peh</u>·cheh·neh <u>seh</u>·slah·nih·noh	roasted with bacon
pečený <u>peh</u>·cheh·nee	baked, roasted
pečený brambor <u>peh</u>·cheh·nee <u>brahm</u>·bohr	roast potato
pečivo <u>peh</u>·chih·voh	pastry
perlička <u>pehr</u>·lihch·kah	guinea fowl
perlivý <u>pehr</u>·lih·vee	carbonated
perník <u>pehr</u>·neek	gingerbread
petrželka <u>peht</u>·rzhehl·kah	parsley
pfeferonka <u>feh</u>·feh·rohn·kah	chili pepper
piškot <u>pihsh</u>·koht	sponge cake

pivo <u>pih</u>·voh	beer
plátek <u>plah</u>·tehk	slice
platýs <u>plah</u>·tees	halibut
plecko plehts·koh	shoulder (cut of meat)
plísňový sýr <u>plees</u>·n'oh·vee seer	blue cheese
plněné papriky v rajčatové omáčce <u>plnyeh</u>·neh pahp·rih·kih <u>vrahy</u>·chah·toh·veh <u>oh</u>·mahch·tseh	stuffed peppers in tomato sauce
plněný <u>plnyeh</u>·nee	stuffed
podmáslí <u>pohd</u>·mahs·lee	buttermilk
poleva <u>poh</u>·leh·vah	icing
polévka <u>poh</u>·lehf·kah	soup
pomazánka z Nivy <u>poh</u>·mah·zahn·kah <u>znih</u>·vih	blue cheese spread
pomeranč <u>poh</u>·meh·rahnch	orange
pomerančová marmeláda <u>poh</u>·meh·rahn·choh·<u>vah mahr</u>·meh·<u>lah</u>·dah	orange marmalade
pomerančový džus <u>poh</u>·meh·rahn·choh·vee dzhoos	orange juice
porce <u>pohr</u>·tseh	portion
pórek <u>poh</u>·rehk	leek
pórková polévka <u>pohr</u>·koh·vah <u>poh</u>·lehf·kah	leek soup
portské víno <u>pohrts</u>·keh <u>vee</u>·noh	port
pražený arašíd <u>prah</u>·zheh·nee ah·rah·sheed	roasted peanut
pražený mandle <u>prah</u>·zheh·nee <u>mahnd</u>·leh	roasted almond
prso prsoh	breast
předrkm przhehdkrm	appetizer
přírodní řízek <u>przhee</u>·rohd·nee <u>rzhee</u>·zehk	unbreaded cutlet
pstruh pstrooh	trout
pstruh na másle pstrooh <u>nah</u>·mah·sleh	trout fried with butter

pudink <u>poo</u>·dihnk	custard
pudinkový krém <u>poo</u>·dihn·koh·vee krehm	cream
punč poonch	punch
rajče <u>rahy</u>·cheh	tomato
rajská omáčka <u>rahy</u>·skah <u>oh</u>·mah·chkah	tomato sauce
rajská polévka <u>rahy</u>·skah <u>poh</u>·lehf·kah	tomato soup
rak rahk	crayfish
ramstejk <u>rahm</u>·stehyk	rumpsteak
rebarbora <u>reh</u>·bahr·boh·rah	rhubarb
rizoto <u>rih</u>·zoh·toh	risotto
rohlík <u>roh</u>·hleek	roll
rosol <u>roh</u>·sohl	aspic
roštěnka <u>rohsh</u>·tyehn·kah	sirloin steak
roštěnky na pivě <u>rohsh</u>·tyehn·kih <u>nah</u>·pih·vyeh	stew of beef and onion cooked in beer
rozinka <u>roh</u>·zihn·kah	raisin
rozmarýna <u>rohz</u>·mah·ree·nah	rosemary
ruláda <u>roo</u>·lah·dah	fillet steak
ruské vejce <u>roos</u>·keh <u>vehy</u>·tseh	eggs with mayonnaise
růžičková kapusta <u>roo</u>·zhihch·koh·vah kah·poos·tah	Brussels sprouts
růžový <u>roo</u>·zhoh·vee	rosé (wine)
ryba <u>rih</u>·bah	fish
rybí filé <u>rih</u>·bee <u>fih</u>·leh	fish fillet
rybí polévka <u>rih</u>·bee <u>poh</u>·lehf·kah	fish soup
rýže <u>ree</u>·zheh	rice
ředkvička <u>rzhehd</u>·kfihch·kah	radish
řeřicha <u>rzheh</u>·rzhih·khah	watercress

řízek <u>rzhee</u>·zehk	cutlet
s citrónem stsih·troh·nehm	with lemon
s cukrem <u>stsook</u>·rehm	with sugar
s ledem <u>sleh</u>·dehm	with ice
s mlékem <u>smleh</u>·kehm	with milk
salám <u>sah</u>·lahm	salami
salát <u>sah</u>·laht	salad, lettuce
salát ze syrového zelí <u>sah</u>·laht zeh <u>sih</u>·roh·veh·hoh <u>zeh</u>·lee	coleslaw
sardelky <u>sahr</u>·dehl·kih	anchovies
sardelová pasta <u>sahr</u>·deh·loh·vah <u>pahs</u>·tah	anchovy paste
sardinka <u>sahr</u>·dihn·kah	sardine
sekaná <u>seh</u>·kah·nah	ground [minced] beef
selátko <u>seh</u>·laht·koh	suckling pig
sendvič <u>sehnd</u>·vihch	sandwich
sirup <u>sih</u>·roop	syrup
sklenice <u>skleh</u>·nih·tseh	glass
skopové <u>skoh</u>·poh·veh	mutton
skopový guláš <u>skoh</u>·poh·vee <u>goo</u>·lahsh	mutton stew
skořice <u>skoh</u>·rzhih·tseh	cinnamon
skotská whisky <u>skoht</u>·skah <u>vihs</u>·kih	Scotch
sladkokyselá omáčka <u>slahd</u>·koh·kih·seh·lah <u>oh</u>·mahch·kah	sweet-and-sour sauce
sladký <u>slahd</u>·kee	sweet
slané mandle <u>slah</u>·neh <u>mahn</u>·dleh	salted almond
slaneček <u>slah</u>·neh·chehk	salted herring
slanina <u>slah</u>·nih·nah	bacon
slaný <u>slah</u>·nee	salty

slávka slahf·kah	mussels
sleď slehdy	herring
slepičí vývar s nudlemi sleh·pih·chee vee·vahr snood·leh·mih	chicken broth with noodles
slivovice slih·voh·vih·tseh	plum brandy
slunečnicová semínka sloo·nehch·nih·tsoh·vah seh·meen·kah	sunflower seeds
smažená ryba smah·zheh·nah rih·bah	fried fish
smažená vejce smah·zheh·nah vehy·tseh	scrambled eggs
smažené kuře smah·zheh·neh koo·rzheh	fried chicken
smaženka smah·zhehn·kah	croquette
smažený smah·zheh·nee	fried
smažený kapr smah·zheh·nee kahpr	carp fried in breadcrumbs
smažený květák s bramborem smah·zheh·nee kfyeh·tahk sbrahm·boh·rehm	cauliflower fried in breadcrumbs
smažený sýr smah·zheh·nee seer	cheese fried in breadcrumbs
smažený vepřový řízek smah·zheh·nee vehp·rzhoh·vee rzhee·zehk	fried pork chop Viennese style
smetana smeh·tah·nah	cream
smetanová omáčka smeh·tah·noh·vah oh·mahch·kah	cream sauce
smetanový smeh·tah·noh·vee	creamy
sněhová pusinka snyeh·hoh·vah poo·sihn·kah	meringue
snídaně snee·dah·nyeh	breakfast
sodovka soh·dohv·kah	soda water
sója soh·yah	soy [soya]
solený soh·leh·nee	salted

solený arašíd <u>soh</u>·leh·nee <u>ah</u>·rah·sheed	salted peanut
specialita dne <u>speh</u>·tsyah·lih·tah dneh	dish of the day
speciality šéfa kuchyně <u>speh</u>·tsyah·lih·tih <u>sheh</u>·fah <u>koo</u>·khih·nyeh	specialties of the house
srdce srtseh	heart
srnčí srnchee	venison
srnčí hřbet dušený na víně srnchee hrzhbeht <u>doo</u>·sheh·nee nah <u>vee</u>·nyeh	fillet of venison braised in wine
stehno <u>steh</u>·hnoh	leg (cut of meat)
stolní víno <u>stohl</u>·nee <u>vee</u>·noh	table wine
strouhanka <u>stroh</u>·hahn·kah	breadcrumbs
strouhaný <u>stroh</u>·hah·nee	grated
studená jídla <u>stoo</u>·deh·nah <u>yeed</u>·lah	cold dishes
studená polévka <u>stoo</u>·deh·nah <u>poh</u>·lehf·kah	cold soup
studená voda <u>stoo</u>·deh·nah <u>voh</u>·dah	iced water
studený <u>stoo</u>·deh·nee	cold
suchý <u>soo</u>·chee	dry
sůl sool	salt
sultánka <u>suhl</u>·tahn·kah	sultana raisin
sušená švestka <u>soo</u>·sheh·nah <u>shfehst</u>·kah	prune
sušené datle <u>soo</u>·sheh·neh <u>daht</u>·leh	dried date
sušenka <u>soo</u>·shehn·kah	cookie [biscuit]
sušený fík <u>soo</u>·sheh·nee feek	dried fig
svíčková <u>sveech</u>·koh·vah	tenderloin (cut of meat)
svíčková na smetaně <u>sveech</u>·koh·vah <u>nah</u>·smeh·tah·nyeh	beef tenderloin in creamy root vegetable sauce
sýr seer	cheese

syrový <u>sih</u>·roh·vee	raw
šafrán <u>shahf</u>·rahn	saffron
šalotka <u>shah</u>·loht·kah	shallot
šalvěj <u>shahl</u>·vyehy	sage
šery <u>sheh</u>·rih	sherry
šípkový čaj <u>sheep</u>·koh·vee chahy	rosehip tea
škubánky s mákem <u>shkoo</u>·bahn·kih <u>smah</u>·kehm	bread dumplings with poppy seeds and sugar
šlehačka <u>shleh</u>·hahch·kah	whipped cream
šopský salát <u>shohps</u>·kee sah·laht	tomato, cucumber and feta cheese salad
špagety <u>shpah</u>·geh·tih	spaghetti
špek shpehk	bacon
špekáčka <u>shpeh</u>·kahch·kah	thin sausage
špekový knedlík se zelím <u>shpeh</u>·koh·vee <u>knehd</u>·leek <u>seh</u>·zeh·leem	dumplings stuffed with bacon, served with sauerkraut
špenát <u>shpeh</u>·naht	spinach
šproty <u>shproh</u>·tih	sprats (small herring)
šťáva <u>shťah</u>·vah	gravy
štika <u>shtih</u>·kah	pike
štrúdl shtroodl	apple strudel
šumivé víno <u>shoo</u>·mih·veh <u>vee</u>·noh	sparkling wine
šumivý <u>shoo</u>·mih·vee	sparkling (drinks)
šunka <u>shoon</u>·kah	ham
šunka od kosti <u>shoon</u>·kah <u>oht</u>·kohs·tih	ham on the bone
šunka s vejci <u>shoon</u>·kah <u>svehy</u>·tsih	ham and eggs
švestka <u>shfehst</u>·kah	plum

švestkové knedlíky shfehst·koh·veh knehd·lee·kih	plum dumplings with curd cheese and sugar
tatarský biftek tah·tahrs·kee beef·tehk	steak tartare
tavený sýr tah·veh·nee seer	soft cheese
telecí teh·leh·tsee	veal
telecí játra teh·leh·tsee yah·trah	veal liver
teplý tehp·lee	warm
těsto tyehs·toh	pastry
těstoviny tyehs·toh·vih·nih	pasta
těžký tyehzh·kee	full-bodied (wine)
tmavý chléb tmah·vee khlehb	dark bread
toast tohst	toast
tonik toh·nihk	tonic water
topinka toh·pihn·kah	toast
tresčí játra trehs·chee yaht·rah	cod liver
treska trehs·kah	cod
třešeň trzheh·shehn'	cherry
tučný tooch·nee	fatty
tuňák too·n'ahk	tuna
turecká káva too·rehts·kah kah·vah	Turkish coffee
tykev tih·kehf	squash
tymián tih·myahn	thyme
uherský salám oo·hehrs·kee sah·lahm	Hungarian salami
úhoř oo·horzh	eel
umělé sladidlo oo·myeh·leh slah·dih·dloh	sweetener
ústřice oos·trzhih·tseh	oyster
utopenci oo·toh·pehn·tsih	sausage marinated in vinegar

uzená makrela <u>oo</u>·zeh·nah mahk·reh·lah	smoked mackerel
uzená šunka <u>oo</u>·zeh·nah <u>shoon</u>·kah	smoked ham
uzenáč <u>oo</u>·zeh·nahch	smoked herring
uzené maso <u>oo</u>·zeh·neh <u>mah</u>·soh	smoked pork
uzené maso se zelím a knedlíky <u>oo</u>·zeh·neh <u>mah</u>·soh seh·zeh·leem ah·knehd·lee·kih	smoked pork with sauerkraut and dumplings
uzený <u>oo</u>·zeh·nee	smoked
uzený búček <u>oo</u>·zeh·nee <u>boo</u>·chehk	smoked pork bacon
uzený jazyk <u>oo</u>·zeh·nee <u>yah</u>·zihk	smoked tongue
uzený losos <u>oo</u>·zeh·nee <u>loh</u>·sohs	smoked salmon
uzený sýr <u>oo</u>·zeh·nee seer	smoked cheese
uzený úhoř <u>oo</u>·zeh·nee <u>oo</u>·hohrzh	smoked eel
vafle <u>vahf</u>·leh	waffle
vaječná jídla <u>vah</u>·yehch·nah yeed·lah	egg dishes
vanilka <u>vah</u>·nihl·kah	vanilla
vanilková zmrzlina <u>vah</u>·nihl·koh·vah <u>zmrzlih</u>·nah	vanilla ice cream
vařené brambory <u>vah</u>·rzheh·neh <u>brahm</u>·boh·rih	boiled potatoes
vařený v páře <u>vah</u>·rzheh·nee <u>fpah</u>·rzheh	steamed
vařící <u>vah</u>·rzhee·tsee	boiling (water)
večeře <u>veh</u>·cheh·rzheh	dinner
vejce <u>vehy</u>·tseh	egg
vepřová klobáska <u>vehp</u>·rzhoh·vah <u>kloh</u>·bahs·kah	pork sausage
vepřové <u>vehp</u>·rzhoh·veh	pork
vepřové žebírko <u>vehp</u>·rzhoh·veh <u>zheh</u>·beer·koh	stewed rib of pork
vermut <u>vehr</u>·moot	vermouth
vídeňská káva <u>vee</u>·dehn's·kah <u>kah</u>·vah	Viennese-style coffee topped with whipped cream

víno <u>vee</u>·noh	wine
višeň <u>vih</u>·shehn'	sour cherry
vlašský ořech <u>vlahsh</u>·skee <u>oh</u>·rzhehkh	walnut
voda <u>voh</u>·dah	water
vuřt voorzht	sausage
vývar <u>vee</u>·vahr	consommé
zajíc <u>zah</u>·yeets	hare
zajíc na divoko <u>zah</u>·yeets <u>nah</u>·dih·voh·koh	hare cooked with bacon, onions and vegetables in red wine
zajíc na smetaně <u>zah</u>·yeets <u>nah</u>·smeh·tah·nyeh	hare in rich cream sauce
zákusek <u>zah</u>·koo·sehk	cake, dessert
zapékaný <u>zah</u>·peh·kah·nee	au gratin
zavináč <u>zah</u>·vih·nahch	pickled herring [rollmop]
zázvor <u>zahz</u>·vohr	ginger
zázvorky <u>zahz</u>·vohr·kih	ginger cookies
zelená paprika <u>zeh</u>·leh·nah <u>pahp</u>·rih·kah	green peppers
zeléňačka zeh·leh·n'ahch·kah	thick soup with potatoes, sauerkraut and cream
zelené fazole <u>zeh</u>·leh·neh <u>fah</u>·zoh·leh	green beans
zelenina <u>zeh</u>·leh·nih·nah	vegetable
zeleninová jídla <u>zeh</u>·leh·nih·noh·vah <u>yeed</u>·lah	vegetable dishes
zeleninová polévka <u>zeh</u>·leh·nih·noh·vah <u>poh</u>·lehf·kah	vegetable soup
zelí <u>zeh</u>·lee	cabbage

zelná polévka s klobásou <u>zehl</u>·nah <u>poh</u>·lehf·kah <u>skloh</u>·bah·soh — cabbage soup with smoked sausage

zmrzlina <u>zmrzlih</u>·nah — ice cream

zmrzlinový pohár (s ovocem) <u>zmrzlih</u>·noh·vee poh·<u>hah</u>r (<u>soh</u>·voh·tsehm) — ice-cream sundae (with fruit)

znojemská pečeně <u>znoh</u>·yehms·kah <u>peh</u>·cheh·nyeh — slices of roast beef in a pickle sauce

zralý <u>zrah</u>·lee — ripe

zvěřina <u>zvyeh</u>·rzhih·nah — game

žampion <u>zhahm</u>·pyohn — champignon mushroom

žebírka <u>zheh</u>·beer·kah — ribs

želé <u>zheh</u>·leh — jelly

žemle <u>zhehm</u>·leh — bun

žitný chléb <u>zhiht</u>·nee khlehb — rye bread

žloutek <u>zhloh</u>·tehk — egg yolk

▼ People

Talking

Essential

Hello./Hi!	**Dobrý den./Nazdar!** <u>dohb</u>·ree dehn/<u>nahz</u>·dahr
How are you?	**Jak se máte?** yahk seh <u>mah</u>·teh
Fine, thanks.	**Dobře, děkuji.** <u>dohb</u>·rzheh dyeh·koo·yih
Excuse me!	**Promiňte!** <u>proh</u>·mihn'·teh
Do you speak English?	**Mluvíte anglicky?** <u>mloo</u>·vee·teh <u>ahn</u>·glihts·kih
What's your name?	**Jak se jmenujete?** yahk seh <u>ymeh</u>·noo·yeh·teh
My name is...	**Jmenuji se...** <u>ymeh</u>·noo·yih seh...
Pleased to meet you.	**Těší mě.** <u>tyeh</u>·shee myeh
Where are you from?	**Odkud jste?** <u>oht</u>·koot ysteh
I'm from *the U.S./ the U.K.*	**Jsem ze Spojených Států/z Velké Británie.** ysehm <u>zeh</u>·<u>spoh</u>·yeh·neekh <u>stah</u>·too/<u>sfehl</u>·keh brih·<u>tah</u>·nyeh
What do you do?	**Čím jste?** cheem ysteh
I work for...	**Pracuji pro...** <u>prah</u>·tsoo·yih proh...
I'm a student.	**Jsem student**♂/**studentka**♀**.** ysehm <u>stoo</u>·dehnt♂/<u>stoo</u>·dehnt·kah♀
I'm retired.	**Jsem v důchodu.** ysehm <u>vdoo</u>·khoh·doo
Do you like...?	**Chcete...?** <u>khtseh</u>·teh...
Goodbye.	**Na shledanou.** <u>nahs</u>·hleh·dah·noh
See you later.	**Na viděnou.** <u>nah</u>·vih·dyeh·noh

Communication Difficulties

Do you speak English?	**Mluvíte anglicky?** mloo·vee·teh ahn·glihts·kih
Does anyone here speak English?	**Mluví tady někdo anglicky?** mloo·vee tah·dih nyehg·doh ahn·glihts·kih
I don't speak much Czech.	**Neumím moc česky.** neh·oo·meem mohts chehs·kih
Could you speak more slowly?	**Můžete mluvit pomaleji?** moo·zheh·teh mloo·viht poh·mah·leh·yih
Could you repeat that?	**Můžete to zopakovat?** moo·zheh·teh toh zoh·pah·koh·vaht
What was that?	**Co jste řekl?** tsoh ysteh rzhehkl
Can you write it down?	**Můžete mi to napsat?** moo·zheh·teh mih toh nahp·saht
Can you translate this for me?	**Můžete mi tohle přeložit?** moo·zheh·teh mih toh·hleh przheh·loh·zhiht
What does *this/ that* mean?	**Co to/tamto znamená?** tsoh toh/tahm·toh znah·meh·nah
I understand.	**Rozumím.** roh·zoo·meem
I don't understand.	**Nerozumím.** neh·roh·zoo·meem
Do you understand?	**Rozumíte?** roh·zoo·mee·teh

You May Hear...

Mluvím jenom trochu anglicky. mloo·veem yeh·nohm troh·khoo ahn·glihts·kih	I only speak a little English.
Nemluvím anglicky. neh·mloo·veem ahn·glihts·kih	I don't speak English.

Making Friends

Hello./Hi!	**Dobrý den./Nazdar!** <u>dohb</u>·ree dehn/<u>nahz</u>·dahr
Good morning.	**Dobré ráno.** <u>dohb</u>·reh <u>rah</u>·noh
Good afternoon.	**Dobré odpoledne.** <u>dohb</u>·reh <u>oht</u>·poh·lehd·neh
Good evening.	**Dobrý večer.** <u>dohb</u>·ree <u>veh</u>·chehr
My name is...	**Jmenuji se...** <u>ymeh</u>·noo·yih seh...
What's your name?	**Jak se jmenujete?** yahk seh <u>ymeh</u>·noo·yeh·teh
I'd like to introduce you to...	**Dovolte, abych Vám představil...** <u>doh</u>·vohl·teh <u>ah</u>·bihkh v**ah**m <u>przhehd</u>·stah·vihl...
Pleased to meet you.	**Těší mě.** <u>tyeh</u>·shee myeh
How are you?	**Jak se máte?** yahk seh <u>mah</u>·teh
Fine, thanks.	**Dobře, děkuji.** <u>dohb</u>·rzheh <u>dyeh</u>·koo·yih
And you?	**A Vy?** ah vih

Upon meeting, men generally shake hands—whether they are meeting for the first time or are old friends. Women shake hands with women and men at the first meeting or in formal situations. Kisses on the cheek are not commonly accepted in the Czech Republic; it is practiced only among close friends.

Travel Talk

I'm here...	**Jsem zde...** ysehm zdeh...
- on business	**- služebně** <u>sloo</u>·zhehb·nyeh
- on vacation [holiday]	**- na dovolené** <u>nah</u>·doh·voh·leh·neh
- studying	**- studuji** <u>stoo</u>·doo·yih
I'm staying for...	**Budu tady...** <u>boo</u>·doo <u>tah</u>·dih...

105

I've been here...	Jsem tady... ysehm <u>tah</u>·dih...
– a day	– **na den** <u>nah</u>·dehn
– a week	– **na týden** <u>nah</u>·tee·dehn
– a month	– **na měsíc** <u>nah</u>·myeh·seets

▶ For numbers, see page 170.

Where are you from?	**Odkud jste?** <u>oht</u>·koot ysteh
I'm from...	**Jsem z...** ysehm s...

Relationships

Who are you with?	**S kým tady jste?** skeem <u>tah</u>·dih ysteh
I'm on my own.	**Jsem tady sám**♂/**sáma**♀. ysehm <u>tah</u>·dih sahm♂/<u>sah</u>·mah♀
I'm with...	**Jsem tady s...** ysehm <u>tah</u>·dih s...
– my *husband/wife*	– **manželem/manželkou** <u>mahn</u>·zheh·lehm/<u>mahn</u>·zhehl·koh
– my *boyfriend/ girlfriend*	– **milencem/milenkou** <u>mih</u>·lehn·tsehm/<u>mih</u>·lehn·koh
– a *friend/colleague*	– **přítelem/kolegou** <u>przhee</u>·teh·lehm/<u>koh</u>·leh·goh
When's your birthday?	**Kdy máte narozeniny?** ghih <u>mah</u>·teh nah·roh·zeh·nih·nih

| How old are you? | **Kolik je vám let?** koh·lihk yeh vahm leht |
| I'm... | **Mne...letý.** mneh...leh·tee |

▶ For numbers, see page 170.

Are you married?	**Jste ženatý♂/vdaná♀?** ysteh zheh·nah·tee♂/vdah·nah♀
I'm...	**Jsem...** ysehm...
– single	– **svobodný♂/svobodná♀** sfoh·bohd·nee♂/sfoh·bohd·nah♀
– married	– **ženatý♂/vdaná♀** zheh·nah·tee♂/vdah·nah♀
– divorced	– **rozvedený♂/rozvedená♀** rohz·veh·deh·nee♂/rohz·veh·deh·nah♀
I'm separated.	**Jsem v separaci.** ysehm fseh·pah·rah·tsih
I'm in a relationship.	**Mám partnera♂/partnerku♀.** mahm pahrt·neh·rah♂/pahrt·nehr·koo♀
I'm widowed.	**Jsem vdovec♂/vdova♀.** ysehm vdoh·vehts♂/vdoh·vah♀
Do you have *children/ grandchildren*?	**Máte *děti/vnuky*?** mah·teh dyeh·tih/vnoo·kih

Work and School

What do you do?	**Čím jste?** cheem ysteh
What are you studying?	**Co studujete?** tsoh stoo·doo·yeh·teh
I'm studying...	**Studuji...** stoo·doo·yih...
I work *full time/ part time*.	**Pracuji v *plném/v polovičním* úvazku.** prah·tsoo·yih fplnehm/fpoh·loh·vihch·neem oo·vahs·koo
Who do you work for?	**Pro koho pracujete?** proh koh·hoh prah·tsoo·yeh·teh

I work for...	**Pracuji pro...** prah·tsoo·yih proh...
Here's my business card.	**Zde je moje vizitka.** zdeh yeh <u>moh</u>·yeh <u>vih</u>·ziht·kah

▶ For business travel, see page 143.

Weather

What's the weather forecast for tomorrow?	**Jaká je předpověď počasí na zítřek?** <u>yah</u>·kah yeh <u>przheht</u>·poh·vyehty <u>poh</u>·chah·see nah <u>zeet</u>·rzhehk
What *beautiful/ terrible* weather!	**Jaké *krásné/ošklivé* počasí!** <u>yah</u>·keh <u>krahs</u>·neh/<u>ohsh</u>·klih·veh <u>poh</u>·chah·see
It's *cool/warm*.	**Je *chladno/teplo*.** yeh <u>khlahd</u>·noh/<u>tehp</u>·loh
It's *rainy/sunny*.	**Je *deštivě/sluneční* počasí.** yeh <u>dehsh</u>·tih·vyeh/<u>sloo</u>·nehch·nee <u>poh</u>·chah·see
It's snowy.	**Sněží.** <u>snyeh</u>·zhee
It's icy.	**Je zima.** yeh <u>zih</u>·mah
Do I need *a jacket/ an umbrella*?	**Budu potřebovat *bundu/deštník*?** <u>boo</u>·doo <u>poht</u>·rzheh·boh·vaht <u>boon</u>·doo/<u>dehsht</u>·neek

▶ For temperature, see page 175.

Romance

Essential

Would you like to go out for a *drink/meal*?	**Nešli bychom si dát *drink/jídlo*?** <u>nesh</u>·lih <u>bih</u>·khohm sih daht *drihnk/<u>jeed</u>·loh*
What are your plans for *tonight/ tomorrow*?	**Jaké máte plány na *dnešní večer/zítřek*?** <u>yah</u>·keh <u>mah</u>·teh <u>plah</u>·nih nah *<u>dnehsh</u>·nee veh·chehr/<u>zeet</u>·rzhehk*

Can I have your number?	**Dáte mi Vaše telefonní číslo?** <u>dah</u>·teh mih <u>vah</u>·sheh <u>teh</u>·leh·fohn·nee <u>chees</u>·loh
Can I join you?	**Můžu se přisednout?** <u>moo</u>·hoo seh <u>przhih</u>·sehd·noht
Can I buy you a drink?	**Mohu Vám objednat něco k pití?** <u>moh</u>·hoo vahm <u>ohb</u>·yehd·naht <u>nyeh</u>·tsoh <u>kpih</u>·tee
I like you.	**Mám tě rád♂/ráda♀.** mahm tyeh rahd♂/<u>rah</u>·dah♀
I love you.	**Miluji tě.** <u>mih</u>·loo·yih tyeh

▶ For formal and informal usage, see page 163.

Making Plans

Would you like to go out for *coffee/dinner*?	**Nešli bychom na *kávu/večeři*?** <u>nehsh</u>·lih <u>bih</u>·khohm <u>nah·kah</u>·voo/<u>veh</u>·cheh·rzhih
What are your plans for...?	**Jaké máte plány na...?** <u>yah</u>·keh <u>mah</u>·teh <u>plah</u>·nih nah...
– tonight	– **dnešní večer** <u>dnehsh</u>·nee veh·chehr
– tomorrow	– **zítřek** <u>zeet</u>·rzhehk
– this weekend	– **víkend** <u>vee</u>·kehnd
Where would you like to go?	**Kam by si chtěl jít?** kahm bih sih khtyehl yeet
I'd like to go to...	**Chtěl♂/Chtěla♀ bych jít do...** khtyehl♂/<u>khtyeh</u>·lah♀ bihkh yeet doh...
Do you like...?	**Chcete...?** <u>khtseh</u>·teh...
Can I have your *number/e-mail*?	**Dáte mi Vaše *telefonní číslo/adresu elektronické pošty*?** <u>dah</u>·teh mih <u>vah</u>·sheh <u>teh</u>·leh·fohn·nee <u>chees</u>·loh/<u>ahd</u>·reh·soo eh·lehk·troh·nihts·keh <u>pohsh</u>·tih

▶ For e-mail and phone, see page 44.

Pick-up [Chat-up] Lines

Can I join you?	**Můžu se přisednout?** <u>moo</u>·zhoo seh przhih·sehd·noht
You're very attractive.	**Vypadáte báječně.** <u>vih</u>·pah·dah·teh <u>bah</u>·yehch·nyeh
Shall we go somewhere quieter?	**Půjdeme někam kde je větší klid?** <u>pooy</u>·deh·meh <u>nyeh</u>·kahm gdeh yeh <u>vyeht</u>·shee klihd

Accepting and Rejecting

Thank you. I'd love to.	**Děkuji. Velice rád♂/ráda♀.** <u>dyeh</u>·koo·yih <u>veh</u>·lih·tseh raht♂/<u>rah</u>·dah♀
Where shall we meet?	**Kde se setkáme?** gdeh seh <u>seht</u>·kah·meh
I'll meet you at *the bar/your hotel.*	**Sejdeme se *v baru/ve vašem hotelu.*** <u>sehy</u>·deh·meh seh *fbah*·roo/<u>veh</u>·vah·shehm hoh·teh·loo
I'll come by at...	**Přijdu v...** <u>przhihy</u>·doo v...
What's your address?	**Kde bydlíte?** gdeh <u>bihd</u>·lee·teh
I'm busy.	**Jsem zaneprázdněný♂/zaneprázdněná♀.** ysehm <u>zah</u>·nehp·rahzd·nyeh·nee♂/ <u>zah</u>·nehp·rahzd·nyeh·nah♀
I'm not interested.	**Nemám zájem.** <u>neh</u>·mahm <u>zah</u>·yehm
Leave me alone, please.	**Nechte mí, prosím.** <u>nekh</u>·teh mee <u>proh</u>·seem
Stop bothering me!	**Ne otravujte mně!** neh <u>oht</u>·rah·vooy·teh mnyeh

Getting Physical

| Can I hug/kiss you? | **Můžu se k tobě přitisknout/tě políbit?** <u>moo</u>·zhoo seh <u>ktoh</u>·byeh <u>przhih</u>·tihs·knoht/tyeh <u>poh</u>·lee·biht |

Yes.	**Ano.** <u>ah</u>·noh
No.	**Ne.** neh
Stop!	**Nech toho!** nehkh <u>toh</u>·hoh

Sexual Preferences

Are you gay?	**Jseš homosexual?** ysehsh <u>hoh</u>·moh·seh·ksoo·ahl
I'm...	**Jsem...** ysehm...
– heterosexual	– **heterosexuální**♂/**heterosexuálná**♀
	<u>heh</u>·teh·roh·seh·ksoo·**ahl**·nee♂/
	<u>heh</u>·teh·roh·seh·ksoo·**ahl**·nah♀
– homosexual	– **homosexuální**♂/**homosexuálná**♀
	<u>hoh</u>·moh·seh·ksoo·**ahl**·nee♂/
	<u>hoh</u>·moh·seh·ksoo·**ahl**·nah♀
– bisexual	– **bisexuální**♂/**bisexuálná**♀
	<u>bih</u>·seh·ksoo·**ahl**·nee♂/
	<u>bih</u>·seh·ksoo·**ahl**·nah♀

▼ Fun

Essential

Where's the tourist information office?	**Kde je turistická kancelář?** gdeh yeh <u>too</u>·rihs·tihts·kah <u>kahn</u>·tseh·lahrzh
What are the main points of interest?	**Co tady stojí za prohlédnutí?** tsoh <u>tah</u>·dih <u>stoh</u>·yee zah <u>proh</u>·hlehd·noo·tee
Are there tours in English?	**Jsou prohlídky s anglickým průvodcem?** ysoh <u>proh</u>·hleet·kih <u>sahn</u>·glihts·keem <u>proo</u>·voht·tsehm
Could I have a *map/guide*?	**Můžete mi dát *mapu/průvodce*?** <u>moo</u>·zheh·teh mih daht <u>mah</u>·poo/<u>proo</u>·vohd·tseh

Tourist Information Office ───────

Do you have any information on...?	**Máte nějaké informace o...?** <u>mah</u>·teh <u>nyeh</u>·yah·keh <u>ihn</u>·fohr·mah·tseh oh...
Can you recommend...?	**Můžete mi doporučit...?** <u>moo</u>·zheh·teh mih <u>doh</u>·poh·roo·chiht...
– a boat trip	– **výlet lodí** <u>vee</u>·leht <u>loh</u>·dee
– an excursion	– **výlet** <u>vee</u>·leht
– a sightseeing tour	– **prohlídku** <u>proh</u>·hleet·koo

Turistické kanceláře (tourist information offices) are usually located in the vicinity of train stations or in city centers. They are open from Monday to Friday and, during the tourist season, also on Saturday and Sunday. Opening hours vary. Some offices, during the tourist season, are open at 7 a.m.; however, the majority operates, from 9 or 10 a.m. to 5 or 6 p.m. Each office can provide extensive information on accommodation, restaurants, sightseeing or city transportation as well as on cultural events taking place in a given town.

Tours

I'd like to go on the tour to...	**Mám zájem o zájezd do...** mahm <u>zah</u>·yehm oh <u>zah</u>·yehzd doh...
When's the next tour?	**Kdy bude další zájezd?** gdyh <u>boo</u>·deh <u>dahl</u>·shee <u>zah</u>·yezd
Are there tours in English?	**Jsou zájezdy s anglickým průvodcem?** ysoh <u>zah</u>·yehz·dih <u>sahn</u>·glihts·keem <u>proo</u>·voht·tsehm
Is there an English-speaking guide?	**Máte průvodce, kteří umí anglicky?** <u>mah</u>·teh <u>proo</u>·voht·tseh <u>kteh</u>·rzhee <u>oo</u>·mee <u>ahn</u>·glihts·kih
What time do we *leave/return*?	**V kolik *vyrazíme/se vrátíme*?** <u>fkoh</u>·lik <u>vih</u>·rah·zee·meh/seh <u>vrah</u>·tee·meh
We'd like to see...	**Rádi bychom viděli...** <u>rah</u>·dih <u>bih</u>·khohm <u>vih</u>·dyeh·lih...
Can we stop here...?	**Mohli bychom tady zastavit na...?** <u>moh</u>·hlih <u>bih</u>·khohm <u>tah</u>·dih zahs·tah·viht nah...
– to take photographs	**– pár fotek** pahr <u>foh</u>·tehk
– to buy souvenirs	**– nákup suvenýrů** <u>nah</u>·koop <u>soo</u>·veh·nee·roo
– to use the restrooms [toilets]	**– záchod** <u>zah</u>·khoht
Is there access for the disabled?	**Je přístup pro invalidy?** yeh <u>przhee</u>·stoop <u>proh</u>·ihn·vah·lih·dih

► For ticketing, see page 18.

Sights

Where *is/are*...?	**Kde *je/jsou*...?** gdeh yeh/ysoh...
– the battleground	**– bitevní pole** <u>bih</u>·tehv·nee <u>poh</u>·leh
– the botanical garden	**– botanická zahrada** <u>boh</u>·tah·nihts·kah <u>zah</u>·hrah·dah
– the castle	**– hrad** hraht

114

– the downtown area	– **centrum** <u>tsehn</u>·troom
– the fountain	– **kašna** <u>kahsh</u>·nah
– the library	– **knihovna** <u>knih</u>·hohv·nah
– the market	– **tržnice** <u>trzhnih</u>·tseh
– the museum	– **muzeum** <u>moo</u>·zeh·oom
– the old town	– **staré město** <u>stah</u>·reh <u>myehs</u>·toh
– the palace	– **palác** <u>pah</u>·lahts
– the park	– **park** pahrk
– the ruins	– **zříceniny** <u>zrzhee</u>·tseh·nih·nih
– the shopping area	– **nákupní centrum** <u>nah</u>·koop·nee <u>tsehnt</u>·room
– the town square	– **náměstí** <u>nah</u>·myehs·tee
Can you show me on the map?	**Můžete mi to ukázat na mapě?** <u>moo</u>·zheh·teh mih toh <u>oo</u>·kah·zaht <u>nah</u>·mah·pyeh

▶ For directions, see page 31.

115

Impressions

It's...	**To je...** toh yeh...
– amazing	– **obdivuhodné** <u>ohb</u>·dih·voo·hohd·neh
– beautiful	– **krásné** <u>krahs</u>·neh
– boring	– **nudné** <u>nood</u>·neh
– interesting	– **zajímavé** <u>zah</u>·yee·mah·veh
– magnificent	– **velkolepé** <u>vehl</u>·koh·leh·peh
– romantic	– **romantické** <u>roh</u>·mahn·tihts·keh
– strange	– **divné** <u>dihv</u>·neh
– stunning	– **skvělé** <u>skfyeh</u>·leh
– terrible	– **strašné** <u>strahsh</u>·neh
– ugly	– **ošklivé** <u>ohsh</u>·klih·veh
I *like/don't like* it.	*Líbí/Nelíbí* se mi to. <u>lee</u>·bee/<u>neh</u>·lee·bee seh mih toh

Religion

Where's...?	**Kde je...?** gdeh yeh...
– the cathedral	– **katedrála** <u>kah</u>·tehd·rah·lah
– the *Catholic/Protestant* church	– **katolický/evangelický kostel** <u>kah</u>·toh·lihts·kee/<u>eh</u>·vahn·geh·lihts·kee <u>kohs</u>·tehl
– the mosque	– **mešita** <u>meh</u>·shih·tah
– the shrine	– **kaple** <u>kahp</u>·leh
– the synagogue	– **synagóga** <u>sih</u>·nah·goh·gah
– the temple	– **chrám** khrahm
What time is *mass/the service*?	**V kolik hodin je *mše/bohoslužba*?** <u>fkoh</u>·lihk <u>hoh</u>·dihn yeh *msheh/<u>boh</u>·hoh·sloozh·bah*

116

Shopping

Essential

Where is the *market/mall [shopping centre]*?	**Kde je *tržnice/nákupní centrum*?** gdeh yeh *trzhnih*·tseh/*nah*·koop·nee *tsehnt*·room	
I'm just looking.	**Jenom se dívám.** yeh·nohm seh dee·vahm	
Can you help me?	**Můžete mi pomoci?** moo·zheh·teh mih poh·moh·tsih	
I'm being helped.	**Již mě obsluhují.** yihzh myeh ohp·sloo·hoo·yee	
How much?	**Kolik?** koh·lihk	
That one.	**Tamten.** tahm·tehn	
That's all, thanks.	**To je všechno, děkuji.** toh yeh vsheh·khnoh dyeh·koo·yih	
Where do I pay?	**Kde zaplatím?** gdeh zah·plah·teem	
I'll pay *in cash/by credit card*.	**Zaplatím *v hotovosti/kreditní kartou*.** zah·plah·teem *fhoh*·toh·voh·stih/*kreh*·diht·nee *kahr*·toh	
A receipt, please.	**Stvrzenku, prosím.** stvrzehn·koo proh·seem	

Stores

Where is...?	**Kde *je/jsou*...?** gdeh yeh/ysoh...
– the antiques store	– **starožitností** stah·roh·zhiht·nohs·tee
– the bakery	– **pekařství** peh·kahrzh·stfee
– the bank	– **banka** bahn·kah
– the bookstore	– **knihkupectví** knihh·koo·pehts·tfee
– the clothing store	– **oděvy** oh·dyeh·vih
– the delicatessen	– **lahůtky** lah·hoot·kih

117

Where is...?	Kde *je/jsou*...? gdeh *yeh/ysoh*...
– the department store	– **obchodní dům** <u>ohp</u>·khohd·nee doom
– the gift shop	– **suvenýry** <u>soo</u>·veh·nee·rih
– the health food store	– **zdravá výživa** <u>zdrah</u>·vah <u>vee</u>·zhih·vah
– the jeweler	– **klenotnictví** <u>kleh</u>·noht·nihts·tfee
– the liquor store [off-licence]	– **obchod lihovinami** <u>ohp</u>·khohd <u>lih</u>·hoh·vih·nah·mih
– the market	– **tržnice** <u>trzhnih</u>·tseh
– the pastry shop	– **cukrárna** <u>tsook</u>·rahr·nah
– the pharmacy [chemist]	– **lékárna** <u>leh</u>·kahr·nah
– the produce [grocery] store	– **potraviny** <u>poht</u>·rah·vih·nih
– the shoe store	– **obuvnictví** <u>oh</u>·boov·nihts·tfee
– the shopping mall [centre]	– **nákupní centrum** <u>nah</u>·koop·nih <u>tsehnt</u>·room
– the souvenir store	– **suvenýry** <u>soo</u>·veh·nee·rih
– the supermarket	– **samoobsluha** <u>sah</u>·moh·ohp·sloo·hah
– the tobacconist	– **tabák** <u>tah</u>·bahk
– the toy store	– **hračkářství** hrahch·kahrzh·stfee

Services

Can you recommend...?	**Můžete mi doporučit...?** <u>moo</u>·zheh·teh mih <u>doh</u>·poh·roo·chiht...
– a barber	– **holičství** <u>hoh</u>·lihch·stfee
– a dry cleaner	– **čistírna** <u>chihs</u>·teer·nah
– a hairdresser	– **kadeřnictví** <u>kah</u>·dehrzh·nihts·tfee

– a laundromat [launderette]	– **prádelna** <u>prah</u>·dehl·nah
– a nail salon	– **manikúru** <u>mah</u>·nih·koo·roo
– a spa	– **spa** spah
– a travel agency	– **cestovní kancelář** <u>tsehs</u>·tohv·nee <u>kahn</u>·tseh·**lahrzh**
Can you...this?	**Můžete to...?** <u>moo</u>·zheh·teh toh...
– alter	– **upravit** <u>oo</u>·prah·viht
– clean	– **vyčistit** <u>vih</u>·chihs·tiht
– mend	– **spravit** <u>sprah</u>·viht
– press	– **vyžehlit** <u>vih</u>·zheh·hliht
When will it be ready?	**Kdy to bude hotové?** gdih toh <u>boo</u>·deh <u>hoh</u>·toh·veh

Spa

I'd like...	**Chtěl**♂/**Chtěla**♀ **bych...** khtyehl♂/ khtyeh·lah♀ bihkh...
- an *eyebrow/ bikini* wax	- **depilaci** *obočí/bikiny* **voskem** deh·pih·lah·tsih oh·boh·chee/bih·kih·nih vohs·kehm
- a facial	- **ošetřit obličej** oh·sheht·rzhiht ohb·lih·chehy
- a *manicure/ pedicure*	- **manikúru/pedikúru** mah·nih·koo·roo/ peh·dih·koo·roo
- a (sports) massage	- **(sportovní) masáž** (spohr·tohv·nee) mah·sahzh
Do you do...?	**Děláte...?** dyeh·lah·teh...
- acupuncture	- **akupunkturu** ah·koo·poon·ktoo·roo
- aromatherapy	- **aromatickou terapii** ah·roh·mah·tihts·koh teh·rah·pyih
- oxygen treatment	- **kyslíkovou terapii** kihs·lee·koh·voh teh·rah·pyih
Is there a sauna?	**Je tady sauna?** yeh tah·dih sow·nah

i

Czech spas are characterized by luxurious facilities, a high level of service and, often, mineral springs. Among the most popular destinations are the southwestern Karlové Vary and Mariánské Lázně.
Luhačovice and Klimkovice attract spa lovers to the region of Moravia, while Karlova Studánka in the heart of the Jesionniki mountains boasts the cleanest air in Central Europe.

Hair Salon

I'd like...	**Chtěl**♂/**Chtěla**♀ **bych...** khtyehl♂/ khtyeh·lah♀ bihkh...
- an appointment for *today/tomorrow*	- **termín na** *dnes/zítřek* tehr·meen nah dnehs/zeet·rzehk
- some color	- **obarvit vlasy** oh·bahr·viht vlah·sih

– some highlights	– **melír** <u>meh</u>·leer
– my hair styled	– **učesat** <u>oo</u>·cheh·saht
– a haircut	– **ostříhat** <u>ohs</u>·trzhee·haht
– a trim	– **zastřihnout** <u>zah</u>·strzhih·noht
Don't cut it too short.	**Nestříhejte mě moc nakrátko.** <u>nehs</u>·trzhee·hehy·teh meyh mohts <u>nah</u>·kraht·koh
Shorter here.	**Tady krátší.** <u>tah</u>·dih <u>kraht</u>·shee

Sales Help

When does...open/ close?	**Kdy...otvírá/zavírá?** gdih...<u>oht</u>·fee·rah/ <u>zah</u>·vee·rah
Where is/are...?	**Kde je/jsou...?** gdeh yeh/ysoh...
– the cashier [cash desk]	– **pokladna** <u>pohk</u>·lahd·nah
– the escalator	– **eskalátor** <u>ehs</u>·kah·lah·tohr
– the elevator [lift]	– **výtah** <u>vee</u>·tah
– the fitting rooms	– **zkušební kabinka** <u>skoo</u>·shehb·nee <u>kah</u>·bihn·kah
– the store directory [guide]	– **informační tabule** <u>ihn</u>·fohr·mahch·nee <u>tah</u>·boo·leh
Can you help me?	**Můžete mi pomoci?** <u>moo</u>·zheh·teh mih poh·moh·tsih
I'm just looking.	**Jenom se dívám.** <u>yeh</u>·nohm seh <u>dee</u>·vahm
I'm being helped.	**Už mě obsluhují.** oozh myeh <u>ohb</u>·sloo·hoo·yee
Do you have any...?	**Máte...?** <u>mah</u>·teh...
Can you show me...?	**Můžete mi ukázat...?** <u>moo</u>·zheh·teh mih oo·kah·zaht...
Can you ship/wrap it?	**Můžete mi to poslat/zabalit?** <u>moo</u>·zheh·teh mih toh <u>pohs</u>·laht/<u>zah</u>·bah·liht
How much?	**Kolik?** <u>koh</u>·lihk

| That's all, thanks. | **To je všechno, děkuji.** toh yeh <u>fshehkh</u>·noh <u>dyeh</u>·koo·yih |

▶ For clothing items, see page 128.

▶ For food items, see page 76.

▶ For souvenirs, see page 124.

You May Hear...

Čím posloužím? cheem <u>pohs</u>·loh·zheem	Can I help you?
Chviličku. <u>khfih</u>·lihch·koo	One moment.
Co byste si přáli? tsoh <u>bihs</u>·teh sih <u>przhah</u>·lih	What would you like?
Ještě něco ? <u>yehsh</u>·tyeh <u>nyeh</u>·tsoh	Anything else?

Preferences

I'd like something...	**Chtěl♂/Chtěla♀ bych ňeco...** khtyehl♂/ khtyeh·lah♀ bihkh <u>n'eh</u>·tsoh...
– cheap/expensive	– **levného/drahého** <u>lehv</u>·neh·hoh/<u>drah</u>·heh·hoh
– larger/smaller	– **většího/menšího** <u>vyeht</u>·shee·hoh/ <u>mehn</u>·shee·hoh
– from this region	– **místního** <u>mees</u>·tnee·hoh
Is it real?	**Je to pravé?** yeh toh <u>prah</u>·veh
Could you show me *this/that*?	**Můžete mi ukázat** *tenhle/tamten*? <u>moo</u>·zheh·teh mih <u>oo</u>·kah·zaht *<u>tehn</u>·hleh/ <u>tahm</u>·tehn*

Decisions

That's not quite what I want.	**Není to úplně ono.** <u>neh</u>·nee toh <u>oopl</u>·nyeh <u>oh</u>·noh

No, I don't like it.	**Ne, to se mi nelíbí.** neh toh seh mih <u>neh</u>·lee·bee
That's too expensive.	**To je moc drahé.** toh yeh mohts <u>drah</u>·heh
I'd like to think about it.	**Ještě si to rozmyslím.** <u>yesh</u>·tyeh sih toh <u>rohz</u>·mihs·leem
I'll take it.	**Vezmu si to.** <u>vehz</u>·moo sih toh

Bargaining

That's too much.	**Je to přiliš drahé.** yeh toh <u>przhih</u>·leesh <u>drah</u>·heh
I'll give you...	**Dám vám...** dahm vahm...
I only have... crowns.	**Mám jenom...korun.** mahm <u>yeh</u>·nohm... <u>koh</u>·roon
Is that your best price?	**To je nejnižší cena?** toh yeh <u>nehy</u>·nihzh·shee <u>tseh</u>·nah
Can you give me a discount?	**Dáte mi nějakou slevu?** <u>dah</u>·teh mih <u>nyeh</u>·yah·koh <u>sleh</u>·voo

▶ For numbers, see page 170.

Paying

How much?	**Kolik?** <u>koh</u>·lihk
I'll pay...	**Zaplatím...** <u>zah</u>·plah·teem...
– in cash	– **hotově** <u>hoh</u>·toh·vyeh
– by credit card	– **kreditní kartou** <u>kreh</u>·diht·nee <u>kahr</u>·toh
– by travelers check [cheque]	– **cestovním šekem** <u>tsehs</u>·tohv·neem <u>sheh</u>·kehm
A receipt, please.	**Stvrzenku, prosím.** <u>stvrzehn</u>·koo <u>proh</u>·seem

i

In some major chain stores (e.g. Delvita) **euro** (bank notes only) are accepted, as are **korun** (Czech crowns) and credit cards. Credit cards are accepted by all major shops and the majority of restaurants, hotels, multiplex movie theaters and certain sports centers. However, in restaurants it is advisable to ask about the minimum amount accepted for payment by card. Travelers checks can be cashed in banks.

You May Hear...

Jak budete platit? yahk <u>boo</u>·deh·teh <u>plah</u>·tiht	How are you paying?
Jenom v hotovostí, prosím. <u>yeh</u>·nohm <u>fhoh</u>·toh·voh·stee <u>proh</u>·seem	Cash only, please.
Nemáte menší drobné? <u>neh</u>·mah·teh <u>mehn</u>·shee <u>drohb</u>·neh	Do you have any smaller change?

Complaints

I'd like...	**Chtěl**♂/**Chtěla**♀ **bych...** khtyehl♂/<u>khtyeh</u>·lah♀ bihkh...
– to exchange this	– **to vyměnit** toh <u>vih</u>·myeh·niht
– to return this	– **to vrátit** toh <u>vrah</u>·tiht
– a refund	– **vrátit peníze** <u>vrah</u>·tiht <u>peh</u>·nee·zeh
– to see the manager	– **mluvit s vedoucím** <u>mloo</u>·viht <u>sfeh</u>·doh·tseem

Souvenirs

Becher® brandy	**Becherovka®** <u>beh</u>·kheh·rohf·kah
bottle of wine	**láhev vína** <u>lah</u>·hehf <u>vee</u>·nah
box of chocolates	**bonboniéra** <u>bohn</u>·boh·nyeh·rah
calendar	**kalendář** <u>kah</u>·lehn·dahrzh

cut crystal	**broušené sklo** <u>broh</u>·sheh·neh skloh
Czech garnets	**České granáty** <u>chehs</u>·keh <u>grah</u>·nah·tih
doll	**panenka** <u>pah</u>·nehn·kah
hand-painted eggs	**velikonoční vajíčka** <u>veh</u>·lih·koh·noch·nee <u>vah</u>·yeech·kah
embroidery	**výšivky** <u>vee</u>·shihf·kih
key ring	**přívěsek ke klíčům** <u>przhee</u>·vyeh·shehk keh·klee·choom
lace	**krajka** <u>krahy</u>·kah
porcelain	**porcelán** <u>pohr</u>·tseh·lahn
postcard	**pohlednica** <u>poh</u>·hlehd·nih·tsah
pottery	**keramika** <u>keh</u>·rah·mih·kah
puppet	**loutka** <u>loht</u>·kah
scarf	**šátek** <u>shah</u>·tehk
souvenir guide	**obrázkový průvodce** <u>ohb</u>·rahs·koh·vee <u>proo</u>·voht·tseh
tea towel	**utěrka** <u>oo</u>·tyehr·kah
T-shirt	**tričko** <u>trihch</u>·koh
wooden toys	**dřevěná hračka** <u>drzheh</u>·vyeh·nah <u>hrahch</u>·kah
Can I see *this/ that*?	**Můžu *to/tamto* vidět?** <u>moo</u>·zhoo toh/<u>tahm</u>·toh vih·dyeht
It's the one in the *window/display case.*	**To je ten z *výlohy/výkladní skříně.*** toh yeh tehn z <u>vee</u>·loh·hih/<u>veek</u>·lahd·nih skrzee·nyeh
I'd like...	**Chtěl♂/Chtěla♀ bych...** khtyehl♂/ <u>khtyeh</u>·lah♀ bihkh...
– a battery	**– baterii** <u>bah</u>·teh·ryih
– a bracelet	**– náramek** <u>nah</u>·rah·mehk
– a brooch	**– brož** brohzh
– earrings	**– náušnice** <u>nah</u>·oosh·nih·tseh

I'd like...	**Chtěl ♂/Chtěla ♀ bych...** khtyehl ♂/ khtyeh·lah ♀ bihkh...
– a necklace	– **náhrdelník** <u>nah</u>·hrdehl·neek
– a ring	– **prsten** prstehn
– a watch	– **hodinky** <u>hoh</u>·dihn·kih
– copper	– **měď** myehdy
– crystal	– **křišťál** <u>krzhih</u>·st'ahl
– diamond	– **diamant** <u>dyah</u>·mahnt
– *white/yellow* gold	– *bílé/žluté* **zlato** <u>bee</u>·leh/<u>zhloo</u>·teh <u>zlah</u>·toh
– pearl	– **perlu** <u>pehr</u>·loo
– pewter	– **cín** tseen
– platinum	– **platina** <u>plah</u>·tih·nah
– sterling silver	– **stříbro** <u>strzheeb</u>·roh
Is this real?	**Je to pravé?** yeh toh <u>prah</u>·veh
Can you engrave it?	**Může se na tom rýt?** <u>moo</u>·zheh seh na tohm reet

i Books about respective regions can be bought in almost all bookstores. There are also many souvenir stands, offering numerous inexpensive gift items. Real treasures can be found at **jarmarki** (fairs): Bohemian cut glass, handmade bells, embroidered tablecloths, folk costumes or plum brandy from a local distillery.

Antiques

How old is this?	**Jak je to staré?** yahk yeh toh <u>stah</u>·reh
Do you have anything from the...era?	**Máte něco z...období?** <u>mah</u>·teh <u>nyeh</u>·tsoh z...<u>ohb</u>·doh·bee
Will I have problems with customs?	**Budu mít problémy na celnici?** <u>boo</u>·doo meet <u>prohb</u>·leh·mih <u>nah</u>·tsehl·nih·tsih
Is there a certificate of authenticity?	**Máte osvědčení pravosti?** <u>mah</u>·teh <u>ohs</u>·fyeht·cheh·nee <u>prah</u>·vohs·tih

Clothing

I'd like...	**Chtěl♂/Chtěla♀ bych...** khtyehl♂/ <u>khtyeh</u>·lah♀ bihkh...
Can I try this on?	**Mohu si to zkusit?** <u>moh</u>·hoo sih toh <u>skoo</u>·siht
It doesn't fit.	**Není mi to dobře.** <u>neh</u>·nee mih toh <u>dohb</u>·rzheh
It's too...	**Je to moc...** yeh toh mohts...
– big	– **velké** <u>vehl</u>·keh
– small	– **malé** <u>mah</u>·leh
– short	– **krátké** <u>kraht</u>·keh
– long	– **dlouhé** <u>dloh</u>·heh
Do you have this in size...?	**Máte to ve velikosti...?** <u>mah</u>·teh toh <u>veh</u>·veh·lih·kohs·tih...

Do you have this in a *bigger/smaller* size?	**Máte to v *větší/menší* velikosti?** <u>mah</u>·teh toh <u>vyeht</u>·shee/<u>mehn</u>·shee <u>veh</u>·lih·kohs·tih

▶ For numbers, see page 170.

You May See...

PÁNSKÉ ODĚVY	men's clothing
ŽENSKÉ ODĚVY	women's clothing
DĚTSKÉ ODĚVY	children's clothing

Color

I'd like something in...	**Chtěl♂/Chtěla♀ bych něco...** khtyehl♂/<u>khtyeh</u>·lah♀ bihkh nyeh·tsoh...
– beige	– **béžový** <u>beh</u>·zhoh·vee
– black	– **černý** <u>chehr</u>·nee
– blue	– **modrý** <u>mohd</u>·ree
– brown	– **hnědý** <u>hnyeh</u>·dee
– gray	– **šedý** <u>sheh</u>·dee
– green	– **zelený** <u>zeh</u>·leh·nee
– orange	– **oranžový** <u>oh</u>·rahn·zhoh·vee
– pink	– **růžový** <u>roo</u>·zhoh·vee
– purple	– **fialový** <u>fyah</u>·loh·vee
– red	– **červený** <u>chehr</u>·veh·nee
– white	– **bílý** <u>bee</u>·lee
– yellow	– **žlutý** <u>zhloo</u>·tee

Clothes and Accessories

backpack	**batoh** <u>bah</u>·toh
belt	**pásek** <u>pah</u>·sehk

bikini	**bikiny** <u>bih</u>·kih·nih
blouse	**blůza** <u>bloo</u>·zah
bra	**podprsenka** <u>poht</u>·prsehn·kah
briefs [underpants]	**spodní kalhotky** <u>spohd</u>·nee <u>kahl</u>·hoht·kih
coat	**kabát** <u>kah</u>·baht
dress	**šaty** <u>shah</u>·tih
hat	**klobouk** <u>kloh</u>·bohk
jacket	**sako** <u>sah</u>·koh
jeans	**džíny** <u>dzhee</u>·nih
pajamas	**pyžamo** <u>pih</u>·zhah·moh
pants [trousers]	**kalhoty** <u>kahl</u>·hoh·tih
pantyhose [tights]	**punčochové kalhoty** <u>poon</u>·choh·khoh·veh <u>kahl</u>·hoh·tih
purse [handbag]	**kabelka** <u>kah</u>·behl·kah
raincoat	**pláštěnka** <u>plah</u>·shtyehn·kah
scarf	**šátek** <u>shah</u>·tehk
shirt	**košile**♂/**blůza**♀ <u>koh</u>·shih·leh♂/<u>bloo</u>·skah♀
shorts	**krátké kalhoty** <u>kraht</u>·keh <u>kahl</u>·hoh·tih
skirt	**sukně** <u>sook</u>·nyeh
socks	**ponožky** <u>poh</u>·nohzh·kih
stockings	**punčochy** <u>poon</u>·choh·khih
suit	**oblek**♂/**kostým**♀ <u>ohb</u>·lek♂/<u>kohs</u>·teem♀
sunglasses	**sluneční brýle** <u>sloo</u>·nehch·nee <u>bree</u>·leh
sweater	**svetr** sfehtr
sweatshirt	**tričko** <u>trihch</u>·koh
swimming trunks	**pánské plavky** <u>pahn</u>·skeh <u>plahf</u>·kih
swimsuit	**dámské plavky** <u>dahm</u>·skeh <u>plahf</u>·kih
T-shirt	**triko** <u>trih</u>·koh
tie	**kravata** <u>krah</u>·vah·tah
underwear	**spodní prádlo** <u>spohd</u>·nee <u>prahd</u>·loh

Fabric

I'd like...	**Chtěl♂/Chtěla♀ bych něco...** khtyehl♂/khtyeh·lah♀ bihkh nyeh·tsoh...
– cotton	**– z bavlny** zbah·vlnih
– denim	**– z džínsoviny** zdzheen·soh·vih·nih
– lace	**– z krajky** skrahy·kih
– leather	**– z kůže** skoo·zheh
– linen	**– ze lnu** zeh·lnoo
– silk	**– z hedvábí** s hehd·vah·bee
– wool	**– z vlny** zvlnih
Is it machine washable?	**Pere se to v pračce?** peh·reh seh toh fprahch·tseh

Shoes

I'd like...	**Chtěl♂/Chtěla♀ bych...** khtyehl♂/khtyeh·lah♀ bihkh...
– high-heeled shoes	**– boty na vysokých podpatcích** boh·tih nah vih·soh·keekh poht·paht·tseekh
– flat shoes	**– boty bez podpatků** behs poht·paht·koo
– boots	**– kotníčkové boty** koht·neech·koh·veh boh·tih
– loafers	**– mokasíny** moh·kah·see·nih
– sandals	**– sandály** sahn·dah·lih
– shoes	**– boty** boh·tih
– slippers	**– papuče** pah·poo·cheh
– sneakers	**– tenisky** teh·nihs·kih
In size...	**Ve velikosti...** veh·veh·lih·kohs·tih...

▶ For numbers, see page 170.

Sizes

small	**malé** <u>mah</u>·leh
medium	**střední** <u>strzhehd</u>·neh
large	**veliké** <u>veh</u>·lih·keh
extra large	**extra veliké** <u>ehks</u>·trah <u>veh</u>·lih·keh
petite	**pro štíhlé** proh <u>shtee</u>·hleh
plus size	**netypické velikosti** <u>neh</u>·tih·pihts·keh <u>veh</u>·lih·kohs·tih

Newsstand and Tobacconist

Do you sell English-language books/newspapers?	**Prodáváte anglické knihy/noviny?** proh·<u>dah</u>·vah·teh ahn·glihts·keh <u>knih</u>·hih/<u>noh</u>·vih·nih
I'd like...	**Chtěl♂/Chtěla♀ bych...** khtyehl♂/<u>khtyeh</u>·lah♀ bihkh...
– candy [sweets]	– **bonbóny** <u>bohn</u>·boh·nih
– chewing gum	– **žvýkačku** <u>zhvee</u>·kahch·koo
– a chocolate bar	– **čokoládu** <u>choh</u>·koh·lah·doo
– a cigar	– **doutník** <u>doht</u>·neek
– a pack/carton of cigarettes	– **krabičku/kartón cigaret** <u>krah</u>·bih·chkoo/<u>kahr</u>·tohn tsih·gah·reht
– a lighter	– **zapalovač** <u>zah</u>·pah·loh·vahch
– a magazine	– **časopis** <u>chah</u>·soh·pihs
– matches	– **zápalky** <u>zah</u>·pahl·kih
– a newspaper	– **noviny** <u>noh</u>·vih·nih
– a road/town map of...	– **mapu cest a dálnic/města...** <u>mah</u>·poo tsehst ah <u>dahl</u>·nihts/<u>myehs</u>·tah...
– a stamp	– **známka** <u>znahm</u>·kah

Photography

I'd like...camera.	**Chtěl**♂/**Chtěla**♀ **bych...fotoaparát.** khtyehl♂/ khtyeh·lah♀ bihkh...<u>foh</u>·toh·ah·pah·**raht**
– an automatic	– **automatický** <u>ow</u>·toh·mah·tihts·kee
– a digital	– **digitální** <u>dih</u>·gih·tahl·nee
– a disposable	– **na jedno použití** <u>nah</u>·yehd·noh <u>poh</u>·oo·zhih·tee
I'd like...	**Chtěl**♂/**Chtěla**♀ **bych...** khtyehl♂/ khtyeh·lah♀ bihkh...
– a battery	– **baterii** <u>bah</u>·teh·ryih
– digital prints	– **digitální printy** <u>dih</u>·gih·tahl·nee <u>prihn</u>·tih
– a memory card	– **paměťovou kartu** <u>pah</u>·myeh·t'oh·voh <u>kahr</u>·too
Can I print digital photos here?	**Můžu si tu vytisknout digitální fotky?** <u>moo</u>·zhoo sih too <u>vih</u>·tihsk·noht <u>dih</u>·gih·tahl·nee <u>foht</u>·kih

Sports and Leisure

Essential

Where's the game?	**Kde se tady hraje?** gdeh seh <u>tah</u>·dih <u>hrah</u>·yeh
Where's...?	**Kde je...?** gdeh yeh...
– the beach	– **pláž** plahzh
– the park	– **park** pahrk
– the pool	– **bazén** bah·zehn
Is it safe to *swim/ dive* here?	**Dá se tady bezpečně *plavat/skákat do vody?*** <u>dah</u> seh <u>tah</u>·dih <u>behs</u>·pehch·nyeh *<u>plah</u>·vaht/ <u>skah</u>·kaht <u>doh</u>·voh·dih*
Can I rent [hire] golf clubs?	**Můžu si vypůjčit golfové hole?** <u>moo</u>·zhoo sih <u>vih</u>·pooy·chiht <u>gohl</u>·foh·veh <u>hoh</u>·leh

How much per hour?	**Kolik se platí za hodinu?** <u>koh</u>·lihk seh <u>plah</u>·tee <u>zah</u>·hoh·dih·noo
How far is it to...?	**Jak je to daleko do...?** yahk yeh toh <u>dah</u>·leh·koh doh...
Can you show me on the map?	**Můžete mi to ukázat na mapě?** <u>moo</u>·zheh·teh mih toh <u>oo</u>·kah·zaht <u>nah</u>·mah·pyeh

Spectator Sports

When's...?	**Kdy se hraje...?** gdih seh <u>hrah</u>·yeh...
– the basketball game	– **basketbalový turnaj** <u>bahs</u>·keht·bah·loh·vee <u>toor</u>·nahy
– the boxing match	– **zápasy v boxu** <u>zah</u>·pah·sih <u>fboh</u>·ksoo
– the cycling race	– **cyklistické závody** <u>tsihk</u>·lihs·tihts·keh <u>zah</u>·voh·dih
– the golf tournament	– **golfový zápas** <u>gohl</u>·foh·vee <u>zah</u>·pahs
– the soccer [football] game	– **fotbalové utkání** <u>foht</u>·bah·loh·veh <u>oot</u>·kah·nee
– the tennis match	– **tenisové utkání** <u>teh</u>·nih·soh·veh <u>oot</u>·kah·nee
– the volleyball game	– **volejbalová utkání** <u>voh</u>·lehy·bah·loh·vah <u>oot</u>·kah·nee
Which teams are playing?	**Které týmy hrají?** <u>kteh</u>·reh <u>tee</u>·mih <u>hrah</u>·yee
Where's...?	**Kde je...?** gdeh yeh...
– the horsetrack	– **koňská dostihová dráha** <u>kohn's</u>·kah <u>doh</u>·stih·hoh·vah <u>drah</u>·hah
– the racetrack	– **závodní dráha** <u>zah</u>·vohd·nee <u>drah</u>·hah
– the stadium	– **stadion** <u>stah</u>·dyohn
Where can I place a bet?	**Kde mohu podat sázku?** gdeh <u>moh</u>·hoo poh·daht <u>sahs</u>·koo

133

i

Czechs are ardent fans of **lední hokej** (ice hockey) and **fotbal** (soccer). Other popular sports include tennis, cycling and, more recently, **kuželky** (bowling) and golf. Fitness centers are in abundance. During the winter, many Czechs enjoy downhill skiing and cross-country skiing, thanks to the number of beautiful mountain ranges in the Czech Republic. These mountains also lend themselves to walking tours, hiking and mountain climbing (for registered climbers or climbing groups only).

Participating

Where's...?	**Kde je...?** gdeh yeh...
– the golf course	– **golfové hřiště** <u>gohl</u>·foh·veh <u>hrzhihsh</u>·tyeh
– the gym	– **tělocvična** <u>tyeh</u>·lohts·fihch·nah
– the park	– **park** pahrk
– the tennis court	– **tenisový kurt** <u>teh</u>·nih·soh·vee koort

How much per...?	**Kolik se platí za...?** <u>koh</u>·lihk seh <u>plah</u>·tee zah...
– day	– **den** dehn
– hour	– **hodinu** <u>hoh</u>·dih·noo
– game	– **hru** hroo
– round	– **kolo** <u>koh</u>·loh
Can I rent [hire]...?	**Můžu si půjčit...?** <u>moo</u>·zhoo sih <u>pooy</u>·chiht...
– golf clubs	– **golfové hole** <u>gohl</u>·foh·veh <u>hoh</u>·leh
– equipment	– **vybavení** <u>vih</u>·bah·veh·nee
– a racket	– **raketu** <u>rah</u>·keh·too

At the Beach/Pool

Where's the *beach/pool*?	**Kde je *pláž/bazén*?** gdeh yeh *plahzh*/<u>bah</u>·zehn
Is there...?	**Je tu...?** yeh too...
– a kiddie [paddling] pool	– **dětský bazén** <u>dyehts</u>·kee bah·zehn
– an *indoor/outdoor* pool	– *krytý/venkovní* **bazén** <u>krih</u>·tee/<u>vehn</u>·kohv·nee bah·zehn
– a lifeguard	– **plavčík** <u>plahf</u>·cheek
Is it safe...here?	**Je tu bezpečně...?** yeh too <u>behs</u>·pehch·nyeh...
– to swim	– **plavat** <u>plah</u>·vaht
– to dive	– **skákat do vody** <u>skah</u>·kaht doh <u>voh</u>·dih
– for children	– **pro děti** proh <u>dyeh</u>·tih

▶ For travel with children, see page 146.

I'd like to rent [hire]...	**Chtěl♂/Chtěla♀ bych si půjčit...** khtyehl♂/<u>khtyeh</u>·lah♀ bihkh sih <u>pooy</u>·chiht...
– a deck chair	– **skládací lehátko** <u>sklah</u>·dah·tsee leh·<u>haht</u>·koh
– diving equipment	– **potápěčskou výstroj** <u>poh</u>·tah·pyehchs·koh <u>vees</u>·trohy

135

I'd like to rent [hire]...	**Chtěl♂/Chtěla♀ bych si půjčit...** khtyehl♂/ khtyeh·lah♀ bikh sih **pooy**·chiht...
– a jet-ski	– **vodní skútr** <u>vohd</u>·nee skootr
– a motorboat	– **motorový člun** <u>moh</u>·toh·roh·vee chloon
– a rowboat	– **lodičku** <u>loh</u>·dihch·koo
– snorkeling equipment	– **šnorchly** <u>shnohr</u>·khlih
– a surfboard	– **surfingové prkno** <u>sehr</u>·fihn·goh·veh prknoh
– a towel	– **ručník** <u>rooch</u>·neek
– an umbrella	– **slunečník** <u>sloo</u>·nehch·neek
– water skis	– **vodní lyže** <u>vohd</u>·nee lih·zheh
For...hours.	**Na...hodin.** <u>nah</u>...hoh·dihn

▶ For numbers, see page 170.

Winter Sports

A lift pass for a day/five days, please.	**Permanentku na vlek** *na den/na pět dní*, **prosím.** <u>pehr</u>·mah·nehnt·koo <u>nah</u>·vlehk *<u>nah</u>·dehn/<u>nah</u>·pyeht* dnee <u>proh</u>·seem
I want to rent [hire]...	**Chtěl♂/Chtěla♀ bych si půjčit...** khtyehl♂/ khtyeh·lah♀ bikh sih **pooy**·chiht...
– boots	– **lyžařské boty** <u>lih</u>·zhahrzh·skeh <u>boh</u>·tih
– a helmet	– **přilbu** <u>przhihl</u>·boo
– poles	– **hole** <u>hoh</u>·leh
– skis	– **lyže** <u>lih</u>·zheh
– a snowboard	– **snowboardové prkno** <u>snoh</u>·boh·ahr·doh·veh prknoh
– snowshoes	– **sněžnice** <u>snyeh</u>·zhnih·tseh
These are too big/small.	**Tyhle jsou moc** *velké/malé.* <u>tih</u>·hleh ysoh mohts *<u>vehl</u>·keh/<u>mah</u>·leh*

Are there lessons?	**Jsou tady cvičné louky?** ysoh <u>tah</u>·dih <u>tsfihch</u>·neh <u>loh</u>·kih
A trail [piste] map, please.	**Dejte mi mapu stezek, prosím.** <u>dehy</u>·teh mih <u>mah</u>·poo <u>steh</u>·zehk <u>proh</u>·seem

 Beskydy, Jeseníky, Krkonoše and Šumava are only four of numerous mountain ranges thriving with wintertime recreation. Snow lovers can enjoy well-kept and well-lit slopes as well as cross-country routes, sleighing routes and ever more modern ski lifts and equipment rentals. Skiing schools operate in almost all centers; there are also special slopes for children or snowboarders. Dedicated skaters can frequent winter stadiums (found in larger cities).

You May See...

LYŽAŘSKÝ VLEK	drag lift
LANOVKA	cable car
SEDAČKOVÝ VLEK	chair lift
SNADNÁ STEZKA	novice
NÁROČNÁ STEZKA	intermediate
VELMI NÁROČNÁ STEZKA	expert
STEZKA ZAVŘENÁ/NEPŘÍSTUPNÁ	trail [piste] closed

In the Countryside

I'd like a map of...	**Chtěl♂/Chtěla♀ bych mapu...** khtyehl♂/ <u>khtyeh</u>·lah♀ bihkh <u>mah</u>·poo...
– this region	**– této oblasti** <u>teh</u>·toh <u>ohb</u>·lahs·tih
– walking routes	**– turistických cest** <u>too</u>·rihs·tihts·keekh tsehst

137

I'd like a map of...	**Chtěl♂/Chtěla♀ bych mapu...** khtyehl♂/khtyeh·lah♀ bikh *mah*·poo...
– bike routes	– **cyklistických stezek** tsihk·lihs·tihts·keekh steh·zehk
– the trails	– **stezek** steh·zehk
Is it *easy/difficult*?	**Je to snadné/náročné?** yeh toh snahd·neh/nah·roch·neh
Is it *far/steep*?	**Je to daleko/srázně?** yeh toh *dah*·leh·koh/srahz·nyeh
How far is it to...?	**Jak je to daleko do...?** yahk yeh toh *dah*·leh·koh doh...
Can you show me on the map?	**Můžete mi to ukázat na mapě?** *moo*·zheh·teh mih toh *oo*·kah·zaht *nah*·mah·pee
I'm lost.	**Ztratil♂/Ztratila♀ jsem se.** strah·tihl♂/strah·tih·lah♀ ysehm seh
Where *is/are*...?	**Kde je/jsou...?** gdeh yeh/ysoh...
– the bridge	– **most** mohst
– the cave	– **jeskyně** yehs·kih·nyeh
– the cliff	– **útes** *oo*·tehs
– the forest	– **les** lehs
– the lake	– **jezero** *yeh*·zeh·roh
– the mountain	– **hora** *hoh*·rah
– the nature reserve	– **přírodní rezervace** *przhee*·rohd·nee reh·zehr·vah·tseh
– the overlook	– **vyhlídková terasa** *vih*·hleed·koh·vah teh·rah·sah
– the park	– **park** pahrk
– the path	– **pěšina** *pyeh*·shih·nah

– the picnic area	– **místo na piknik** <u>mees</u>·toh nah·<u>pihk</u>·nihk
– the river	– **řeka** <u>rzheh</u>·kah
– the sea	– **moře** <u>moh</u>·rzheh
– the thermal springs	– **termální zřídla** <u>tehr</u>·mahl·nee <u>zrzhee</u>·dlah
– the stream	– **potok** <u>poh</u>·tohk
– the valley	– **údolí** <u>oo</u>·doh·lee
– the vineyard	– **vinice** <u>vih</u>·nih·tseh
– the waterfall	– **vodopád** <u>voh</u>·doh·pahd

Culture and Nightlife

Essential

What is there to do in the evenings?	**Co se tady dá dělat večer?** tsoh seh <u>tah</u>·dih dah <u>dyeh</u>·laht <u>veh</u>·chehr
Do you have a program of events?	**Jaký je program?** <u>yah</u>·kee yeh <u>prohg</u>·rahm
What's playing at the movies [cinema] tonight?	**Co dnes večer hrají v kině?** tsoh dnehs <u>veh</u>·chehr <u>hrah</u>·yee <u>fkih</u>·nyeh
Where's...?	**Kde je...?** gdeh yeh...
– the downtown area	– **centrum** <u>tsehn</u>·troom
– the bar	– **bar** bahr
– the dance club	– **diskotéka** <u>dihs</u>·koh·teh·kah
Is there an admission charge?	**Platí se tam vstupné?** <u>plah</u>·tee seh tahm <u>vstoop</u>·neh

While in the Czech Republic, it is a must to see at least one of the country's 12 sites on the UNESCO World Heritage list: Prague Castle and the city's Old and New Towns; Český Krumlov (one of the largest palace complexes in Europe), Telč (Renaissance city houses); John of Nepomuk Church (18th century) in Zelená Hora; St Barnaby's cathedral (14th-16th century) in Kutná Hora and its old town; Lednicko-Valtický palace and park complex; complete village architecture in the style of folk Baroque in Holašovice; historical residence of bishops and archbishops of Olomouc in Kroměříž (castle surrounded by gardens); 16th century Renaissance castle in Litomyšl; Baroque column of Holy Trinity in Olomouc; Tugendhat villa (20th c) in Brno; and St Prokop basilica and Jewish quarter in Třebíč.

Entertainment

Can you recommend...?	**Můžete mi doporučit...?** <u>moo</u>·zheh·teh mih <u>doh</u>·poh·roo·chiht...
– a concert	**– koncert** <u>kohn</u>·tsehrt
– a movie	**– film** fihlm
– an opera	**– operu** <u>oh</u>·peh·roo
– a play	**– představení** <u>przheht</u>·stah·veh·nee
When does it *start/end*?	**V kolik se *začíná/končí*?** fkoh·lihk seh <u>zah</u>·chee·nah/<u>kohn</u>·chee
I like...	**Mám moc rád♂/ráda♀...** mahm mohts raht♂/rah·dah♀...
– classical music	**– klasickou hudbu** <u>klah</u>·sih·tskoh <u>hood</u>·boo
– folk music	**– lidovou hudbu** <u>lih</u>·doh·voh <u>hood</u>·boo
– jazz	**– džez** dzhehz
– pop music	**– pop** pohp
– rap	**– rap** rahp

▶ For ticketing, see page 18.

You May Hear...

Vypněte mobily, prosím. vihp·nyeh·teh moh·bih·lih proh·seem

Turn off your cell [mobile] phones, please.

Nightlife

What is there to do in the evenings?	**Co se tady dá dělat večer?** tsoh seh tah·dih dah dyeh·laht veh·chehr
Can you recommend...?	**Můžete mi doporučit...?** moo·zheh·teh mih doh·poh·roo·chiht...
– a bar	– **bar** bahr
– a casino	– **kasino** kah·sih·noh
– a dance club	– **diskotéky** dihs·koh·teh·kih
– a gay club	– **klub pro homosexuály** kloop proh hoh·moh·seh·ksoo·ah·lih
– a nightclub	– **noční klub** nohch·nee kloop
Is there live music?	**Je tam živá hudba?** yeh tahm zhih·vah hood·bah
How do I get there?	**Jak se tam dostanu?** yahk seh tahm dohs·tah·noo
Is there an admission charge?	**Platí se tam vstupné?** plah·tee seh tahm fstoop·neh
Let's go dancing.	**Pojďme si tančit.** pohy·dymeh sih tahn·chiht

There are plenty of clubs in large cities, especially in Prague, Brno and Ostrava. Ostrava boasts an entire street with clubs, called Stodolní. The offering is wide—from dance to jazz and other music clubs—and hours are extensive (usually from early evening to early morning). It is advisable to have some form of ID (e.g. driver's license) while traveling at night.

▼ Special Needs

Business Travel

Essential

I'm here on business.	**Jsem tady služebně.** ysehm <u>tah</u>·dih sloo·zhehb·nyeh
Here's my business card.	**Zde je moje vizitka, prosím.** zdeh yeh <u>moh</u>·yeh <u>vih</u>·ziht·kah <u>proh</u>·seem
Can I have your card?	**Můžu Vás poprosit o vaši vizitku?** <u>moo</u>·zhoo vahs <u>poh</u>·proh·siht oh <u>vah</u>·shih <u>vih</u>·ziht·koo
I have a meeting with...	**Mám setkání s...** mahm <u>seht</u>·kah·nee s...
Where's...?	**Kde je...?** gdeh yeh...
– the business center	– **byznysové centrum** <u>bihz</u>·nih·soh·veh tsehn·troom
– the convention hall	– **konferenční sál** <u>kohn</u>·feh·rehnch·nee sahl
– the meeting room	– **jednací síň** <u>yehd</u>·nah·tsee seen'

Business Communication

I'm here to attend...	**Přijel♂/Přijela♀ jsem na...** <u>przhih</u>·yehl♂/ przhih·yeh·lah♀ ysehm nah...
– a seminar	– **seminář** <u>seh</u>·mih·narhz
– a conference	– **konferenci** <u>kohn</u>·feh·rehn·tsih
– a meeting	– **setkání** seht·kah·nee
My name is...	**Jmenuji se...** <u>ymeh</u>·noo·yih seh...
May I introduce my colleague...	**Dovolte, abych Vám představil svého kolegu...** <u>doh</u>·vohl·teh <u>ah</u>·bih vahm <u>przhehd</u>·stah·vihl sveh·hoh koh·leh·goo...
I have *a meeting/ an appointment* with...	***Mám setkání/Jsem domluvený s...*** mahm seht·kah·nee/ysehm <u>dohm</u>·loo·veh·nee s...

I'm sorry I'm late.	**Promiňte, že jdu pozdě.** <u>proh</u>·mihn'·teh <u>zheh</u> ydoo <u>pohzh</u>·dyeh
I need an interpreter.	**Chtěl**♂/**Chtěla**♀ **bych tlumočníka.** khtyehl♂/<u>khtyeh</u>·lah♀ bihkh <u>tloo</u>·mohch·nee·kah
You can reach me at the...Hotel.	**Můžete mne najít v...Hotelu.** <u>moo</u>·zheh·teh mneh <u>nah</u>·yeet f...<u>hoh</u>·teh·loo
I'm here until...	**Zdržím se tady do...** zdrzheem seh <u>tah</u>·dih doh...

 There are two forms of addressing people in Czech. The first, **Pane/Paní** (sir/madam) or **Vy** (formal you) is used with professionals, elderly people and those whom you do not know well. The informal **ty** (you) is used with young people, children and close acquaintances. Using first names in semi-formal contacts is acceptable only if the name is preceded by **Pane/Paní**.

I need to...	**Potřebuji...** <u>poh</u>·trzheh·boo·yih...
– make a call	– **zavolat** <u>zah</u>·voh·laht
– make a photocopy	– **udělat xerokopie** <u>oo</u>·dyeh·laht <u>kseh</u>·roh·koh·pyeh
– send an e-mail	– **poslat e-mail** <u>pohs</u>·laht <u>eh</u>·mehyl
– send a fax	– **faxovat** <u>fah</u>·ksoh·vaht
– send a package (overnight)	– **poslat balík (přes noc)** <u>pohs</u>·laht <u>bah</u>·leek (przhehs nohts)
It was a pleasure to meet you.	**Těší mě.** <u>tyeh</u>·shee myeh

▶ For internet and communications, see page 44.

You May Hear...

Máte domluvené setkání? <u>mah</u>·teh <u>doh</u>·mloo·veh·neh <u>seht</u>·kah·nee	Do you have an appointment?
S kým? skeem	With whom?
Je na schůzi. yeh nah <u>skhoo</u>·zee	*He/She* is in a meeting.
Okamžik, prosím. <u>oh</u>·kahm·zhihk <u>proh</u>·seem	One moment, please.
Posaďte se, prosím. <u>poh</u>·sahdy·teh seh <u>proh</u>·seem	Have a seat.
Dáte si něco k pití? <u>dah</u>·teh sih <u>nyeh</u>·tsoh <u>kpih</u>·tee	Would you like something to drink?
Děkuji za příchod. <u>dyeh</u>·koo·yih zah <u>przhee</u>·khohd	Thank you for coming.

Essential

Is there a discount for children?	**Je na děti sleva?** yeh <u>nah</u>·dyeh·tih <u>sleh</u>·vah
Can you recommend a babysitter?	**Můžete mi doporučit opatrovnice?** <u>moo</u>·zheh·teh mih <u>doh</u>·poh·roo·chiht oh·paht·rohv·nih·tseh
Could we have a *highchair/child's seat*?	**Můžeme dostat *židličku/židli pro dítě*?** <u>moo</u>·zheh·meh <u>dohs</u>·taht *zhih·dlih·chkoo/ zhih·dlih proh <u>dee</u>·tyeh*
Where can I change the baby?	**Kde mohu přebalit dítě?** gdeh <u>moh</u>·hoo <u>przheh</u>·bah·liht <u>dee</u>·tyeh

Fun with Kids

Can you recommend something for the kids?	**Můžete mi doporučit někoho na hlídání děti?** <u>moo</u>·zheh·teh mih <u>doh</u>·poh·roo·chiht nyeh·koh·hoh nah <u>hlee</u>·dah·nee dyeh·tih
Where's...?	**Kde je...?** gdeh yeh...
– the amusement park	– **lunapark** <u>loo</u>·nah·pahrk
– the arcade	– **prostor s hracími automaty** <u>prohs</u>·tohr <u>shrah</u>·tsee·mih <u>ow</u>·toh·mah·tih
– the kiddie [paddling] pool	– **dětský bazén** <u>dyeht</u>·skee <u>bah</u>·zehn
– the park	– **park** pahrk
– the playground	– **dětské hřiště** <u>dyeht</u>·skeh <u>hrzhihsh</u>·tyeh
– the zoo	– **zoo** zoh
Are kids allowed?	**Děti mohou vstoupit?** <u>dyeh</u>·tih <u>moh</u>·hoh <u>fstoh</u>·piht

| Is it safe for kids? | **Je to bezpečné pro děti?** yeh toh <u>behs</u>·pehch·neh proh·dyeh·tih |
| Is it suitable for...year olds? | **Je to vhodné pro...letý?** yeh toh <u>fhohd</u>·neh proh...leh·tee |

▶ For numbers, see page 170.

You May Hear...

Jak je roztomilé! yahk yeh <u>rohz</u>·toh·mih·leh	How cute!
Jak se jmenuje? yahk seh <u>ymeh</u>·noo·yeh	What's *his/her* name?
Kolik je mu let? <u>koh</u>·lihk yeh moo leht	How old is *he/she*?

Basic Needs for Kids

Do you have...?	**Máte...?** <u>mah</u>·teh...
– a baby bottle	– **dětskou láhev s dudlíkem** <u>dyeht</u>·skoh <u>lah</u>·hehf <u>sdood</u>·lee·kehm
– baby wipes	– **navlhčené ubrousky** <u>nahv</u>l·hcheh·neh <u>oo</u>·broh·skih
– a car seat	– **autosedačku** <u>ow</u>·toh·seh·dahch·koo
– a children's menu/portion	– **jídelník pro děti/dětskou porci** <u>yee</u>·dehl·neek proh dyeh·tih/<u>dyeht</u>·skoh pohr·tsih
– a child's seat/ highchair	– **židli pro dítě/židličku** <u>zhih</u>·dlih proh dee·tyeh/<u>zhih</u>·dlih·chkoo
– a crib/cot	– **kolébku/skládací postel** <u>koh</u>·lehp·koo/<u>sklah</u>·dah·tsee pohs·tehl
– diapers [nappies]	– **plenky** <u>plehn</u>·kih
– formula	– **dětskou směs** <u>dyeht</u>·skoh smyehs
– a pacifier [soother]	– **dudlík** <u>dood</u>·leek

147

Do you have...?	**Máte...?** <u>mah</u>·teh...
– a playpen	– **ohrádku** <u>oh</u>·hrahd·koo
– a stroller [pushchair]	– **kočárek** <u>koh</u>·chah·rehk
Can I breastfeed the baby here?	**Můžu zde kojit dítě?** <u>moo</u>·zhoo zdeh <u>koh</u>·yiht <u>dee</u>·tyeh
Where can I change the baby?	**Kde mohu přebalit dětí?** gdeh <u>moh</u>·hoo <u>przheh</u>·bah·liht <u>dyeh</u>·tee

▶ For dining with kids, see page 58.

Babysitting

Can you recommend a reliable babysitter?	**Můžete mi doporučit spolehlivou opatrovnice?** <u>moo</u>·zheh·teh mih <u>doh</u>·poh·roo·chiht <u>spoh</u>·leh·hlih·voh <u>oh</u>·paht·rohv·nih·tseh
What's the charge?	**Kolik to stojí?** <u>koh</u>·lihk toh <u>stoh</u>·yih
We'll be back by...	**Vrátíme se do...** <u>vrah</u>·tee·meh seh doh...

▶ For time, see page 172.

I can be reached at...	**Můžete mě volat na číslo...** <u>moo</u>·zheh·teh myeh <u>voh</u>·laht nah <u>chees</u>·loh...

Health and Emergency

Can you recommend a pediatrician?	**Můžete mi doporučit nějakého pediatru?** <u>moo</u>·zheh·teh mih <u>doh</u>·poh·roo·chiht <u>nyeh</u>·yah·keh·hoh peh·dyaht·roo
My child is allergic to...	**Moje dítě má alergii na...** <u>moh</u>·yeh <u>dee</u>·tyeh mah <u>ah</u>·lehr·gyih nah...
My child is missing.	**Moje dítě se ztratilo.** <u>moh</u>·yeh <u>dee</u>·tyeh seh <u>strah</u>·tih·loh
Have you seen a *boy/girl*?	**Neviděl jste *chlapce/děvčátko*?** <u>neh</u>·vih·dyehl ysteh <u>khlahp</u>·tseh/<u>dyehf</u>·chah·tkoh

▶ For health, see page 154.

▶ For police, see page 152.

For the Disabled

Essential

Is there...?	**Je zde...?** yeh zdeh...
– access for the disabled	– **přístup pro tělesně postižené** <u>przhee</u>·stoop proh <u>tyeh</u>·lehs·nyeh <u>pohs</u>·tih·zheh·neh
– a wheelchair ramp	– **podjezd pro invalidní vozíky** <u>pohd</u>·yehzd proh <u>ihn</u>·vah·lihd·nee <u>voh</u>·zee·kih
– a handicapped- [disabled-] accessible toilet	– **toalety pro tělesně postižené** <u>toh</u>·ah·leh·tih proh <u>tyeh</u>·lehs·nyeh <u>pohs</u>·tih·zheh·neh
I need...	**Potřebuji...** <u>poh</u>·trzheh·boo·yih...
– assistance	– **pomoc** <u>poh</u>·mohts
– an elevator [lift]	– **výtah** <u>vee</u>·tah
– a ground-floor room	– **pokoj v přízemí** <u>poh</u>·kohy <u>fprzee</u>·zeh·mih

149

Getting Help

I'm disabled.	**Jsem tělesně postižený**♂/**postižená**♀. ysehm <u>tyeh</u>·lehs·nyeh <u>pohs</u>·tih·zheh·nee♂/ <u>pohs</u>·tih·zheh·nah♀
I'm deaf.	**Jsem hluchý**♂/**hluchá**♀. ysehm <u>hloo</u>·khee♂/ <u>hloo</u>·khah♀
I'm *visually/ hearing* impaired.	**Špatně** *vidím/slyším.* <u>shpaht</u>·nyeh <u>vih</u>·deem/ <u>slih</u>·sheem
I'm unable to *walk far/use the stairs.*	**Nemůžu** *moc chodit/používat schody.* <u>neh</u>·moo·zhoo mohts <u>khoh</u>·diht/ <u>poh</u>·oo·zhee·vaht <u>skhoh</u>·dih
Can I bring my wheelchair?	**Můžu být na invalidním vozíku?** <u>moo</u>·zhoo beet nah <u>ihn</u>·vah·leed·neem <u>voh</u>·zee·koo
Are guide dogs permitted?	**Můžu přijít s mým psem-průvodcem?** <u>moo</u>·zhoo <u>przhih</u>·yeet smeem psehm <u>proo</u>·vohd·tsehm
Can you help me?	**Můžete mi pomoci?** <u>moo</u>·zheh·teh mih <u>poh</u>·moh·tsih
Please *open/hold* the door.	*Otevřte/Podržte* **dveře, prosím.** <u>oh</u>·teh·vrzhteh/ <u>pohd</u>·rzhteh <u>dveh</u>·rzheh <u>proh</u>·seem

Resources

Emergencies

Essential

Help!	**Pomoc!** <u>poh</u>·mohts
Go away!	**Jděte pryč!** <u>ydyeh</u>·teh prihch
Stop, thief!	**Zastavte zloděje!** <u>zahs</u>·tahf·teh <u>zloh</u>·dyeh·yeh
Get a doctor!	**Zavolejte lékaře!** <u>zah</u>·voh·lehy·teh <u>leh</u>·kah·rzheh
Fire!	**Hoří!** <u>hoh</u>·rzhee
I'm lost.	**Ztratil**♂**/Ztratila**♀ **jsem se.** <u>strah</u>·tihl♂/ <u>strah</u>·tih·lah♀ ysehm seh
Can you help me?	**Můžete mi pomoci?** <u>moo</u>·zheh·teh mih <u>poh</u>·moh·tsih

Police

Essential

Call the police!	**Zavolejte policii!** <u>zah</u>·voh·lehy·teh <u>poh</u>·lih·tsyih
Where's the police station?	**Kde je policejní stanice?** gdeh yeh <u>poh</u>·lih·tsehy·nee <u>stah</u>·nih·tseh
There's been an *accident/attack*.	**Došlo k této *události/útoku*.** <u>doh</u>·shloh <u>kteh</u>·toh <u>oo</u>·dah·lohs·tih/<u>oo</u>·toh·koo
My child is missing.	**Moje dítě se ztratilo.** <u>moh</u>·yeh dee·tyeh seh <u>strah</u>·tih·loh
I need...	**Potřebuji...** <u>poh</u>·trzheh·boo·yih...
– an interpreter	– **tlumočníka** <u>tloo</u>·mohch·nee·kah
– to contact my lawyer	– **se spojit s mým právníkem** seh <u>spoh</u>·yiht smeem <u>prahv</u>·nee·kehm

– to make a phone call	– **zavolat** <u>zah</u>·voh·laht
I'm innocent.	**Jsem nevinný**♂/**nevinná**♀. ysehm <u>neh</u>·vihn·nee♂/<u>neh</u>·vihn·nah♀

You May Hear...

Vyplňte prosím tento formulář. <u>vihpl</u>·n'teh <u>proh</u>·seem <u>tehn</u>·toh <u>fohr</u>·moo·<u>lahrz</u>	Please fill out this form.
Doklad totožnosti, prosím. <u>dohk</u>·lahd toh·tohzh·nohs·tih <u>proh</u>·seem	Your ID, please.
Kdy/Kde se to stalo? gdih/gdeh seh toh <u>stah</u>·loh	*When/Where* did it happen?
Jak *on* **vypadal**♂/*ona* **vypadala**♀? yahk on vih·pah·<u>dahl</u>♂/<u>oh</u>·nah vih·pah·dah·<u>lah</u>♀	What does *he/she* look like?

Lost Property and Theft

I want to report...	**Chtěl**♂/**Chtěla**♀ **bych ohlásit...** khtyehl♂/<u>khtyeh</u>·lah♀ bihkh <u>oh</u>·hlah·siht...
– a mugging	– **přepadení** <u>przheh</u>·pah·deh·nee
– a rape	– **znásilnění** <u>znah</u>·sihl·nyeh·nee
– a theft	– **krádež** <u>krah</u>·dehzh
I've been *robbed/ mugged*.	*Okradli/přepadli* **mě.** <u>oh</u>·krahd·lih/<u>przheh</u>·pahd·lih myeh
I've lost my...	*Ztratil*♂/*Ztratila*♀ **jsem...** <u>strah</u>·tihl♂/<u>strah</u>·tih·lah♀ ysehm...
My...has been stolen.	**Ukradli mi...** <u>oo</u>·krahd·lih mih...
– backpack	– **batoh** <u>bah</u>·toh
– bicycle	– **kolo** <u>koh</u>·loh

My...has been stolen.	**Ukradli mi...** <u>oo</u>·krahd·lih mih...
– camera	– **fotoaparát** <u>foh</u>·toh·ah·pah·raht
– cell [mobile] phone	– **mobilní telefon** <u>moh</u>·bihl·nee <u>teh</u>·leh·fohn
– (rental) car	– **auto (z půjčovny)** <u>ow</u>·toh (<u>spooy</u>·chohv·nih)
– computer	– **počítač** <u>poh</u>·chee·tahch
– credit card	– **kreditní kartou** <u>kreh</u>·diht·nee <u>kahr</u>·toh
– jewelry	– **šperky** <u>shpehr</u>·kih
– money	– **peníze** <u>peh</u>·nee·zeh
– passport	– **pas** pahs
– purse [handbag]	– **kabelku** <u>kah</u>·behl·koo
– travelers check [cheque]	– **cestovní šeky** <u>tsehs</u>·tohv·nee shehk
– wallet	– **peněženku** <u>peh</u>·nyeh·zhehn·koo
I need a police report for my insurance.	**Potřebuji zprávu od policie pro pojišťovnu.** <u>poht</u>·rzheh·boo·yih <u>sprah</u>·voo <u>oht</u>·poh·lih·tsyeh <u>proh</u>·poh·yihsh·t'ohv·noo

Health

Essential

I'm sick [ill].	**Jsem nemocný♂/nemocná♀.** ysehm <u>neh</u>·mohts·nee♂/<u>neh</u>·mohts·nah♀
I need an English-speaking doctor.	**Potřebuji lékaře, který mluví anglicky.** <u>poht</u>·rzheh·boo·yih <u>leh</u>·kah·rzheh <u>kteh</u>·ree <u>mloo</u>·vee <u>ahn</u>·glihts·kih
It hurts here.	**Tady to bolí.** <u>tah</u>·dih toh <u>boh</u>·lee
I have a stomachache.	**Bolí mí břicho.** <u>boh</u>·lee mee <u>brzhih</u>·khoh

Finding a Doctor

Can you recommend a *doctor/dentist*?	**Můžete mi doporučit *lékaře/zubáře*?** moo·zheh·teh mih doh·poh·roo·chiht leh·kah·rzheh/zoo·bah·rzheh
Could the doctor come to see me here?	**Mohl by mě lékař navštívit tady?** mohl bih myeh leh·kahrzh nahf·shtee·viht tah·dih
What are the office hours?	**V kolik přijímá?** fkoh·lihk przhih·yee·mah
Can I make an appointment...?	**Mohu se objednat termín...?** moh·hoo seh ohb·yehd·naht tehr·meen...
– for today	– **na dnešek** nah·dneh·shehk
– for tomorrow	– **na zítra** nah·zeet·rah
– as soon as possible	– **co nejdříve** tsoh nehy·drzhee·veh
It's urgent.	**Je to naléhavé.** yeh toh nah·leh·hah·veh

Symptoms

I'm bleeding.	**Jsem krvácení.** ysehm krfah·tseh·nee
I'm...	**Mám...** mahm...
– dizzy	– **závratě hlavy** zah·vrah·tyeh hlah·vih
– constipated	– **zácpu** zah·tspoo
– nauseous	– **nevolnosti** neh·vohl·nohs·tih
I'm vomiting.	**Zvracím.** zvrah·tseem
It hurts here.	**Tady to bolí.** tah·dih toh boh·lee
I have...	**Mám...** mahm...
– an allergic reaction	– **alergii** ah·lehr·gyih
– a chest pain	– **bolesti v hrudniku** boh·lehs·tih fhrood·nih·koo

I have...	**Mám...** mahm...
- an earache	- **bolest ucha** <u>boh</u>·lehst <u>oo</u>·khah
- a fever	- **horečku** <u>hoh</u>·rehch·koo
- pain	- **bolesti** <u>boh</u>·lehs·tih
- a rash	- **vyrážku** <u>vih</u>·rahzh·koo
- a sprain	- **vyvrtnutí** <u>vih</u>·vrtnoo·tee
- some swelling	- **otok** <u>oh</u>·tohk
- a stomachache	- **bolesti břicha** <u>boh</u>·lehs·tih <u>brzhih</u>·khah
- sunstroke	- **úžeh** <u>oo</u>·zhehh
I've been sick [ill] for...days.	**Jsem nemocný♂/nemocná♀ již...dni.** ysehm <u>neh</u>·mohts·nih♂/<u>neh</u>·mohts·nah♀ yihzh...dnih

▶ For numbers, see page 170.

Health Conditions

I'm...	**Jsem...** ysehm...
- anemic	- **anemik** <u>ah</u>·neh·mihk
- diabetic	- **diabetik** <u>dyah</u>·beh·tihk
- asthmatic	- **astmatik** <u>ahst</u>·mah·tihk
I'm allergic to *antibiotics/ penicillin.*	**Jsem alergický na *antibiotika/ penicillin.*** ysehm <u>ah</u>·lehr·gihts·kee nah <u>ahn</u>·tih·byoh·tih·kah/<u>peh</u>·nih·tsih·lihn

▶ For food items, see page 76.

I have *arthritis/ (high/low) blood pressure.*	**Mám *artritida/(vysoký/nízký) tlak.*** mahm <u>ahrt</u>·rih·dih·tah/(<u>vih</u>·soh·kee/<u>nihs</u>·kee) tlahk
I have a heart condition.	**Mám srdeční potíže.** mahm <u>srdehch</u>·nee poh·tee·zheh
I'm on...	**Užívám...** <u>oo</u>·zhih·vahm...

You May Hear...

Co se stalo? tsoh seh <u>stah</u>·loh — What's wrong?

Kde to bolí? gdeh toh <u>boh</u>·lee — Where does it hurt?

Bolí to tady? <u>boh</u>·lee toh <u>tah</u>·dih — Does it hurt here?

Užíváte nějaké jiné léky? <u>oo</u>·zhee·vah·teh <u>nyeh</u>·yah·keh <u>yih</u>·neh <u>leh</u>·kih — Are you taking any other medication?

Jste na něco alergický♂/alergická♀? ysteh <u>nah</u>·nyeh·tsoh <u>ah</u>·lehr·gihts·kee♂/<u>ah</u>·lehr·gihts·kah♀ — Are you allergic to anything?

Otevřete ústa. <u>oh</u>·teh·frzheh·teh <u>oo</u>·stah — Open your mouth.

Dýchejte zhluboka. <u>dee</u>·hehy·teh <u>shloo</u>·boh·kah — Breathe deeply.

Jdi do nemocnice. ydih doh <u>neh</u>·mohts·nih·tseh — Go to the hospital.

Hospital

Notify my family. — **Uvědomte laskavě mou rodinu.** <u>oo</u>·vyeh·dohm·teh <u>lahs</u>·kah·vyeh moh <u>roh</u>·dih·noo

I'm in pain. — **Mám bolesti.** mahm <u>boh</u>·lehs·tih

I need a *doctor/ nurse*. — **Potřebuji *lékaře/zdravotní sestru*.** <u>poht</u>·rzheh·boo·yih *<u>leh</u>·kah·rzheh/ <u>zdrah</u>·voht·nee sehs·troo*

When are visiting hours? — **Kdy jsou návštěvní hodiny?** gdih ysoh <u>nahf</u>·shtyehv·nee <u>hoh</u>·dih·nih

I'm visiting... — **Jdu navštívit...** ydoo <u>nahf</u>·shtee·viht...

Dentist

I've broken a tooth. — **Udrobil se mi zub.** <u>oo</u>·droh·bihl seh mih zoop

I've lost a filling. — **Vypadla mi plomba.** <u>vih</u>·pahd·lah mih <u>plohm</u>·bah

I have a toothache.	**Bolí mě zub.** <u>boh</u>·lee myeh zoop
Can you fix this denture?	**Můžete mi opravit protézu?** <u>moo</u>·zheh·teh mih <u>oh</u>·prah·viht <u>proh</u>·teh·zoo

Gynecologist

I have *menstrual cramps/a vaginal infection*.	**Mám *bolestivou menstruaci/vaginální infekci*.** mahm <u>boh</u>·lehs·tih·voh <u>mehn</u>·stroo·ah·tsih/ <u>vah</u>·gih·nahl·nee ihn·fehk·tsih
I missed my period.	**Menstuace se mi opožďuje.** <u>mehn</u>·stroo·ah·tseh seh mih <u>oh</u>·pohzh·dyoo·yeh
I'm on the pill.	**Beru antikoncepční pilulky.** <u>beh</u>·roo <u>ahn</u>·tih·kohn·tsehp·chnee pih·lool·kih
I'm (not) pregnant.	**(Ne) Jsem těhotná.** (neh) ysehm <u>tyeh</u>·hoht·nah
I haven't had my period for...months.	**Už...měsícú jsem neměla menstruace.** oozh...<u>myeh</u>·see·tsoo ysehm <u>neh</u>·myeh·lah <u>mehn</u>·stroo·ah·tseh

▶ For numbers, see pake 170.

Optician

I've lost...	**Ztratil♂/Ztratila♀ jsem...** <u>strah</u>·tihl♂/ <u>strah</u>·tih·lah♀ ysehm...
– a contact lens	**– jednu kontaktní čočku** <u>yehd</u>·noo <u>kohn</u>·tahkt·nee <u>chohch</u>·koo
– my glasses	**– brýle** <u>bree</u>·leh
– a lens	**– čočky** <u>chohch</u>·kih

Payment and Insurance

How much?	**Kolik?** <u>koh</u>·lihk
Can I pay by credit card?	**Mohu zaplatit kreditní kartou?** <u>moh</u>·hoo <u>zah</u>·plah·tiht <u>kreh</u>·diht·nee <u>kahr</u>·toh

158

| I have insurance. | **Mám pojištění.** mahm <u>poh</u>·yihsh·tyeh·nee |
| Can I have a receipt for my insurance? | **Mohu dostat stvrzenku pro pojišťovnu?** <u>moh</u>·hoo <u>dohs</u>·taht <u>stvrzehn</u>·koo <u>proh</u>·poh·yihsh·t'ohv·noo |

Pharmacy [Chemist]

Essential

Where's the nearest pharmacy [chemist's]?	**Kde je nejbližší lékárna?** gdeh yeh <u>nehy</u>·blihzh·shee <u>leh</u>·kahr·nah
What time does the pharmacy [chemist's] open/close?	**V kolik *otvírají/zavírají* lékárnu?** <u>fkoh</u>·lihk *<u>oht</u>·fee·rah·yee/<u>zah</u>·vee·rah·yee* <u>leh</u>·kahr·noo
What would you recommend for...?	**Jaký lék byste mi doporučil na...?** <u>yah</u>·kee lehk <u>bihs</u>·teh mih <u>doh</u>·poh·roo·chihl nah...
How much should I take?	**Kolik mám užívat?** <u>koh</u>·lihk mahm <u>oo</u>·zhee·vaht
Can you fill [make up] this prescription for me?	**Můžete mi vydat léky na tento předpis?** <u>moo</u>·zheh·teh mih <u>vih</u>·daht <u>leh</u>·kih <u>nah</u>·tehn·toh <u>przheht</u>·pihs
I'm allergic to...	**Mám alergii na...** mahm <u>ah</u>·lehr·gyih nah...

Pharmacies are marked with a green or white cross and the inscription **Lékárna.** They are generally open from Monday to Friday between 8 a.m. and 6 p.m., and on Saturday until noon. On the door of each pharmacy is a notice as to which pharmacy has extended hours. Not all pharmacies accept credit cards; it is therefore advisable to have cash handy.

Dosage Instructions

How much should I take?	**Kolik mám užívat?** <u>koh</u>·lihk mahm <u>oo</u>·zhee·vaht
How many times a day do I take it?	**Kolikrát denně to mám užívat?** <u>koh</u>·lihk·raht <u>dehn</u>·hyeh toh mahm <u>oo</u>·zhee·vaht
Is it suitable for children?	**Je to vhodné pro děti?** yeh toh <u>vhohd</u>·neh <u>proh</u>·dyeh·tih
I'm taking...	**Beru...** <u>beh</u>·roo...
Are there side effects?	**Mají vedlejší účinki?** <u>mah</u>·yee <u>vehd</u>·lehy·shee <u>oo</u>·chihn·kih

You May See...

JEDENKRÁT/TŘIKRÁT DENNĚ	once/three times a day
TABLETY	tablets
KAPKA	drop
TABLETY/PILULKY	tablets/pills
LŽIČKY	teaspoons

160

PŘED/PO/S JÍDLEM — *before/after/with meals*

NALAČNO — on an empty stomach

SPOLKNĚTE V CELKU — swallow whole

MŮŽE ZPŮSOBIT OSPALOST — may cause drowsniness

POUZE PRO VNĚJŠÍ POUŽITÍ — for external use

Health Problems

I'd like some medicine for... **Chtěl♂/Chtěla♀ bych nějaký lék na...** khtyehl♂/khtyeh·lah♀ bihkh <u>nyeh</u>·yah·kee lehk nah...

- a cold — **rýmu** <u>ree</u>·moo
- a cough — **kašel** <u>kah</u>·shehl
- diarrhea — **průjem** <u>proo</u>·yehm
- insect bites — **štípance** <u>shtee</u>·pahn·tseh
- motion [travel] sickness — **cestovní nemoc** <u>tsehs</u>·tohv·nee <u>neh</u>·mohts
- a sore throat — **bolení v krku** <u>boh</u>·leh·nee fkrkoo
- sunburn — **spálení sluncem** <u>spah</u>·leh·nee <u>sloon</u>·tsehm
- an upset stomach — **bolení břicha** <u>boh</u>·leh·nee <u>brzhih</u>·khah

Basic Needs

I'd like... **Chtěl♂/Chtěla♀ bych...** khtyehl♂/khtyeh·lah♀ bihkh...

- acetaminophen [paracetamol] — **paracetamol** <u>pah</u>·rah·tseh·tah·mohl
- antiseptic cream — **antiseptický krém** <u>ahn</u>·tih·sehp·tihts·kee krehm
- aspirin — **aspirin** <u>ahs</u>·pih·rihn
- a bandage [plaster] — **obinadlo** <u>oh</u>·bih·nahd·loh
- a comb — **hřeben** <u>hrzheh</u>·behn

I'd like...	Chtěl♂/Chtěla♀ bych... khtyehl♂/ khtyeh·lah♀ bihkh...
– condoms	– **kondomy** <u>kohn</u>·dohm
– contact lens solution	– **roztok na čočky** <u>rohs</u>·tohk <u>nah</u>·choh·chkih
– deodorant	– **deodorant** <u>deh</u>·oh·doh·rahnt
– a hairbrush	– **kartáč na vlasy** <u>kahr</u>·tahch <u>nah</u>·vlah·sih
– hair spray	– **lak na vlasy** lahk <u>nah</u>·vlah·sih
– ibuprofen	– **ibuprofén** <u>ih</u>·boo·proh·fehn
– insect repellent	– **repelent proti hmyzu** <u>reh</u>·peh·lehnt <u>proh</u>·tih hmih·zoo
– a nail file	– **pilník na nehty** <u>pihl</u>·neek nah <u>neh</u>·htih
– a (disposable) razor	– **(jednoúčelový) holicí strojek** (<u>yehd</u>·noh·**oo**·cheh·loh·vee) <u>hoh</u>·lih·tsee <u>stroh</u>·yehk
– razor blades	– **žiletky** <u>zhih</u>·leht·kih
– sanitary napkins [pads]	– **dámské vložky** <u>dahm</u>·skeh <u>vlohsh</u>·kih
– shampoo/ conditioner	– **šampon/kondicionér** <u>shahm</u>·pohn/ <u>kohn</u>·dih·tsyoh·**nehr**
– soap	– **mýdlo** <u>meed</u>·loh
– sunscreen	– **krém na opalování** krehm <u>nah</u>·oh·pah·loh·vah·nee
– tampons	– **tampony** <u>tahm</u>·poh·nih
– tissues	– **papírové kapesníky** <u>pah</u>·pee·roh·veh <u>kah</u>·pehs·nee·kih
– toilet paper	– **toaletní papír** <u>toh</u>·ah·leht·nee <u>pah</u>·peer
– a toothbrush	– **kartáček na zuby** <u>kahr</u>·tah·chek <u>nah</u>·zoo·bih
– toothpaste	– **zubní pastu** <u>zoob</u>·nee pahs·too

▶ For baby products, see page 147.

Reference

Grammar

In Czech, there are two forms for you: **ty** (singular) and **vy** (plural). These are used when talking to relatives, close friends and children as well as among young people. When addressing someone in a formal situation use the formal **Vy**.

Regular Verbs

Czech verbs are conjugated based on person, number, tense and gender. The infinitive of most Czech verbs ends in **–t**.
There are four regular conjugation patterns for Czech verbs. The following present, past and future forms of the verbs **dělat** (to do), **vidět** (to see), **nést** (to take) and **kupovat** (to buy) represent these four patterns.

DĚLAT (to do)		Present	Past	Future
I	já	děl**ám**	děl**al jsem** ♂ děl**ala jsem** ♀	budu dělat
you (sing., inf.)	ty	děl**áš**	děl**al jsi** ♂ děl**ala jsi** ♀	budeš dělat
he/she/it	on/ona/ono	děl**á**	děl**al** ♂ děl**ala** ♀ děl**alo** (neuter)	bude dělat
we	my	děl**áme**	děl**ali jsme** ♂ děl**aly jsme** ♀	budeme dělat
you (pl./fml.)	vy/Vy	děl**áte**	děl**ali jste** ♂ děl**aly jste** ♀	budete dělat
they	oni ♂/ony ♀/ ona (neuter)	děl**ají**	děl**ali** ♂ děl**aly** ♀ děl**ala** (neuter)	budou dělat

sing. = singular   pl. = plural   inf. = inf.   fml. = formal

VIDĚT (to see)		Present	Past	Future
I	já	vidím	viděl jsem♂ viděla jsem♀	budu vidět
you (sing., inf.)	ty	vidíš	viděl jsi♂ viděla jsi♀	budeš vidět
he/she/it	on/ona/ono	vidí	viděl♂ viděla♀ vidělo (neuter)	bude vidět
we	my	vidíme	viděli jsme♂ viděly jsme♀	budeme vidět
you (pl./fml.)	vy/Vy	vidíte	viděli jste♂ viděly jste♀	budete vidět
they	oni♂/ony♀/ ona (neuter)	vidí	viděli♂ viděly♀ viděla (neuter)	budou vidět

NÉST (to take)		Present	Past	Future
I	já	nesu	nesl jsem♂ nesla jsem♀	budu nést
you (sing., inf.)	ty	neseš	nesl jsi♂ nesla jsi♀	budeš nést
he/she/it	on/ona/ono	nese	nesl♂ nesla♀ neslo (neuter)	bude nést
we	my	neseme	nesli jsme♂ nesly jsme♀	budeme nést
you (pl./fml.)	vy/Vy	nesete	nesli jste♂ nesly jste♀	budete nést
they	oni♂/ony♀/ ona (neuter)	nesou	nesli♂ nesly♀ nesla (neuter)	budou nést

KUPOVAT (to buy)		Present	Past	Future
I	já	kupuji	kupoval **jsem**♂ kupovala **jsem** ♀	budu kupovat
you (sing., inf.)	ty	kupuješ	kupoval **jsi**♂ kupovala **jsi** ♀	budeš kupovat
he/she/it	on/ona/ono	kupuje	kupoval ♂ kupovala ♀ kupoval**o** (neuter)	bude kupovat
we	my	kupuj**eme**	kupoval**i jsme**♂ kupoval**y jsme** ♀	bude**me** kupovat
you (pl./fml.)	vy/Vy	kupuj**ete**	kupoval**i jste**♂ kupoval**y jste** ♀	bude**te** kupovat
they	oni♂/ony♀/ ona (neuter)	kupuj**í**	kupoval**i**♂ kupoval**y** ♀ kupoval**a** (neuter)	bude**ou** kupovat

Irregular Verbs

Irregular verbs are not conjugated by following the normal rules and, therefore, must be memorized. Following are two common irregular verbs, **być** (to be) and **iść** (to go):

BYĆ (to be)		Present	Past	Future
I	já	jsem	byl jsem♂ byla jsem ♀	budu
you (sing., inf.)	ty	jsi	byl jsi♂ byla jsi ♀	budeš
he/she/it	on/ona/ono	je	byl♂ byla ♀ bylo (neuter)	bude
we	my	jsme	byli jsme♂ byly jsme ♀	budeme
you (pl./fml.)	vy/Vy	jste	byli jste♂ byly jste ♀	budete
they	oni♂/ony♀/ ona (neuter)	jsou	byli♂ byly ♀ byla (neuter)	budou

JÍT (to go)		Present	Past	Future
I	já	jdu	šel jsem ♂ šla jsem ♀	budu jít
you (sing., inf.)	ty	jdeš	šel jsi ♂ šla jsi ♀	budeš jít
he/she/it	on/ona/ono	jde	šel ♂ šla ♀ šlo (neuter)	bude jít
we	my	jdeme	šli jsme ♂ šly jsme ♀	budeme jít
you (pl./fml.)	vy/Vy	jdete	šli jste ♂ šly jste ♀	budete jít
they	oni ♂/ony ♀/ ona (neuter)	jdou	šli ♂ šly ♀ šla (neuter)	budou jít

Nouns

Nouns in Czech are either masculine, feminine or neuter. Masculine nouns usually end in a consonant (**student**, student; **muž**, man). Few of them have the ending –a (**kolega**, friend; **turista**, tourist). Feminine nouns usually end in –a (**žena**, woman), –e (**růže**, rose) or a consonant (**radost**, joy; **povodeň**, flood). Neuter nouns end in –o (**město**, city), –í (**náměstí**, town square) or –e (**pole**, field). Most masculine and feminine nouns, when plural, end in –i or in –y, respectively; most neuter nouns end with –a in the plural.

The endings of nouns vary according to their role in the sentence. There are seven different cases (roles) in both the singular and plural.

There are no articles (a, an, the) in Czech.

Word Order

Word order in Czech is usually as in English, i.e., subject-verb-object. However, word order can be more flexible, because the word ending (case) indicates the role of each word in the sentence.
Example: **Jana dala knihu Karlovi. = Jana dala Karlovi knihu.** (Jana gave Karel a book.)

To ask a question in Czech:

1. invert the subject and the verb
Example: **To je pan Novák.** This is Mr. Novák. **Je to pan Novák?** Is this Mr. Novák?

2. add a rising intonation to an affirmative statement
Example: **Pan Novák?** Mr. Novák?

3. use question words
kde (where, place), **kam** (where, direction), **kdy** (when), **kdo** (who), **co** (what)
Example:
Kde jsi? Where are you?
Kam jdeš? Where are you going?
Kdy se vrátíš? When are you coming back?
Kdo to je? Who is it?
Co budeme dělat? What are we going to do?

Negation

To form a negative sentence, add **ne** (not) before the verb.
Example:
Mám lístek. I have a ticket. **Nemám lístek.** I don't have a ticket.

Imperatives

Imperative sentences are formed by adding the appropriate ending to the verb stem.

Example: Go!

you	ty	Jdi!
he/she/it	on/ona/ono	Ať jde!
we	my	Jděme!
you (pl./fml.)	vy/Vy	Jděte!
they	oni♂/ony♀/ona (neuter)	Ať jdou!

Adjectives

There are two groups of adjectives: strong and weak. Strong adjectives end in hard consonants or vowels –ý ♂, –á ♀, –é (neuter). Soft adjectives end in soft consonants or –í in the nominative (subject) case.

Adjectives must agree in gender, number and case with the nouns they modify.

Example:	strong adjective		weak adjective	
masculine	český student	Czech student	moderní dům	modern house
feminine	česká žena	Czech woman	moderní škola	modern school
neuter	české město	Czech city	moderní auto	modern car

Comparative and Superlative

The comparative is constructed by adding –ejší, –ější to adjectives ending in –ský, –lý, –pý, –vý, –ný, –tý, –rý, and the ending –ší to adjectives ending in –bý, –dý, –hý, –chý, –ký, –oký, –eký. The superlative is formed by adding nej– to the comparative. Example:

levný (cheap)	levnější (cheaper)	nejlevnější (cheapest)
slabý (weak)	slabší (weaker)	nejslabší (weakest)

Pronouns

Pronouns, like nouns, decline according to gender, number and case. Personal pronouns (I, you, he, she, etc.) can look very different from their base forms according to what "role" they play in the sentence.

I	já
you (sing., inf.)	ty
he, she, it	on/ona/ono
we	my
you (pl./fml.)	vy/Vy
they	oni♂/ony♀/ona (neuter)

Possessive Adjectives

	masculine	feminine	neuter
my	můj	moje	moje
your (sing.)	tvůj	tvoje	tvoje
his/her	jeho	jeho	jeho
its	její	její	její
our	náš	naše	naše
your (pl.)	váš	vaše	vaše
their	jejich	jejich	jejich

Example:
To je můj dům. This is my house.
To je moje kniha. This is my book.
To je moje dítě. This is my child.

Adverbs

Most adverbs are derived from the corresponding adjectives by means of special suffixes:

adjectives	adverbs
1. –ý	–e
rychlý (fast)	rychle
2. –ý	–ě
špatný (bad)	špatně
3. –ský, –zký, –cký	–sky, –zky, –cky
český (Czech)	česky
hezký (pretty)	hezky
4. –ý	–o
chladný (cool)	chladno

Numbers

Essential

0	**nula**	<u>noo</u>·lah
1	**jedna**	<u>yehd</u>·nah
2	**dva**	dvah
3	**tři**	trzhih
4	**čtyři**	<u>chtih</u>·rzhih
5	**pět**	pyeht
6	**šest**	shehst
7	**sedm**	sehdm
8	**osm**	ohsm
9	**devět**	<u>deh</u>·vyeht
10	**deset**	<u>deh</u>·seht
11	**jedenáct**	<u>yeh</u>·deh·nahtst
12	**dvanáct**	<u>dvah</u>·nahtst
13	**třináct**	<u>trzhih</u>·nahtst
14	**čtrnáct**	chtrnahtst
15	**patnáct**	<u>paht</u>·nahtst
16	**šestnáct**	<u>shehst</u>·nahtst
17	**sedmnáct**	<u>sehdm</u>·nahtst
18	**osmnáct**	<u>ohsm</u>·nahtst
19	**devatenáct**	<u>deh</u>·vah·teh·nahtst
20	**dvacet**	<u>dvah</u>·tseht
21	**dvacet jedna**	<u>dvah</u>·tseht <u>yehd</u>·nah
22	**dvacet dva**	<u>dvah</u>·tseht dvah
30	**třicet**	<u>trzhih</u>·tseht

31	**třicet jedna** <u>trzhih</u>·tseht <u>yehd</u>·nah
40	**čtyřicet** <u>chtih</u>·rzih·tseht
50	**padesát** <u>pah</u>·deh·saht
60	**šedesát** <u>sheh</u>·deh·saht
70	**sedmdesát** <u>sehdm</u>·deh·saht
80	**osmdesát** <u>ohsm</u>·deh·saht
90	**devadesát** <u>deh</u>·vah·deh·saht
100	**sto** stoh
101	**sto jedna** stoh <u>yehd</u>·nah
200	**dvě stě** dvyeh styeh
500	**pět set** pyeht seht
1,000	**tisíc** <u>tih</u>·seets
10,000	**deset tisíc** <u>deh</u>·seht tih·seets
1,000,000	**milión** <u>mih</u>·lih·ohn

Ordinal Numbers

first	**první** prvnee
second	**druhý** <u>droo</u>·hee
third	**třetí** <u>trzheh</u>·tee
fourth	**čtvrtý** chtfrtee
fifth	**pátý** <u>pah</u>·tee
once	**jednou** <u>yehd</u>·noh
twice	**dvakrát** <u>dvahk</u>·raht
three times	**třikrát** <u>trzhihk</u>·raht

Time

Essential

What time is it?	**Kolik je hodin?** <u>koh</u>·lihk yeh <u>hoh</u>·dihn
It's noon [midday].	**Je dvanáct hodin poledne.** yeh <u>dvah</u>·nahtst <u>hoh</u>·dihn <u>poh</u>·lehd·neh
It's midnight.	**Je půlnoc.** yeh <u>pool</u>·nohts
From 9 o'clock to 5 o'clock.	**Od deváté do páté.** <u>ohd</u>·deh·vah·teh <u>doh</u>·pah·teh
twenty after [past] four	**za deset minut půl páté** <u>zah</u>·deh·seht <u>mih</u>·noot pool <u>pah</u>·teh
a quarter to nine	**tři čtvrtě na devět** trzhih <u>chtvur</u>·tyeh <u>nah</u>·deh·vyeht
5:30 a.m./p.m.	**půl šesté/sedmnáct třicet** pool <u>shehs</u>·teh/ <u>sehdm</u>·nahtst <u>tzhih</u>·tseht

Czechs use the 24-hour clock when writing time, especially in schedules. Morning hours from 1:00 to noon are the same as in English. After noon, 12 should be added to the time: 1 p.m. is 13:00, 6 p.m. is 18:00, etc.

Days

Essential

Monday	**pondělí** <u>pohn</u>·dyeh·lee
Tuesday	**úterý** <u>oo</u>·teh·ree
Wednesday	**středa** <u>strzheh</u>·dah
Thursday	**čtvrtek** chtfrtehk

Friday	**pátek** <u>pah</u>·tehk
Saturday	**sobota** <u>soh</u>·boh·tah
Sunday	**neděle** <u>neh</u>·dyeh·leh

Dates

yesterday	**včera** <u>fcheh</u>·rah
today	**dnes** dnehs
tomorrow	**zítra** <u>zeet</u>·rah
day	**den** dehn
week	**týden** <u>tee</u>·dehn
month	**měsíc** <u>myeh</u>·seets
year	**rok** rohk

Months

January	**leden** <u>leh</u>·dehn
February	**únor** <u>oo</u>·nohr
March	**březen** <u>brzheh</u>·zehn
April	**duben** <u>doo</u>·behn
May	**květen** <u>kfyeh</u>·tehn
June	**červen** <u>chehr</u>·vehn
July	**červenec** <u>chehr</u>·veh·nets
August	**srpen** srpehn
September	**září** <u>zah</u>·rzhee
October	**říjen** <u>rzhee</u>·yehn
November	**listopad** <u>lih</u>·stoh·paht
December	**prosinec** <u>proh</u>·sih·nehts

Seasons

spring	**jaro** <u>yah</u>·roh
summer	**léto** <u>leh</u>·toh
fall [autumn]	**podzim** <u>pohd</u>·zihm
winter	**zima** <u>zih</u>·mah

Holidays

January 1	**Nový Rok, Den vzniku samostatného** New Year's Day, Czech Independence Day
March/April (movable)	**Velikonoce** Easter
May 1	**Svátek práce** Labor Day
May 8	**Den osvobození od fašismu** Victory over Fascism (Liberation Day)
July 5	**Den slovanských věrozvěstů Cyrila a Metoděje** Day of the Slavic Apostles Cyril and Methodius
July 6	**Mistr Jan Hus** Jan Hus Day
November 17	**Dne boje za svobodu a demokracii** Freedom and Democracy Day
December 25	**Sváty vánoční** Christmas Day
December 26	**svätého Štefana** Feast of St. Stephen

Main public holidays in the Czech Republic are connected with recent historical events, such as the liberation after the World War II or restoration of the Czech Republic after the break from Slovakia. Czechs usually spend holidays with their families and friends, enjoying leisure time in town or the countryside.

Conversion Tables

Mileage

1 km – 0.62 mi	20 km – 12.4 mi
5 km – 3.10 mi	50 km – 31.0 mi
10 km – 6.20 mi	100 km – 61.0 mi

Measurement

1 gram	**gram** grahm	= 0.035 oz.
1 kilogram (kg)	**kilo** <u>kee</u>·loh	= 2.2 lb
1 liter (l)	**litr** leetr	= 1.06 U.S./0.88 Brit. quarts
1 centimeter (cm)	**centimetr** tsehn·<u>tyh</u>·mehtr	= 0.4 inch
1 meter (m)	**metr** mehtr	= 3.28 feet
1 kilometer (km)	**kilometr** kee·<u>loh</u>·mehtr	= 0.62 mile

Temperature

-40° C – -40° F	-1° C – 30° F	20° C – 68° F
-30° C – -22° F	0° C – 32° F	25° C – 77° F
-20° C – -4° F	5° C – 41° F	30° C – 86° F
-10° C – 14° F	10° C – 50° F	35° C – 95° F
-5° C – 23° F	15° C – 59° F	

Oven Temperature

100° C – 212° F	177° C – 350° F
121° C – 250° F	204° C – 400° F
149° C – 300° F	260° C – 500° F

Useful Websites

www.czech.cz
official website of the Czech Republic

www.discoverczech.com
hotels, guided tours, car rental, sights

www.hihostels.com
Hostelling International website

www.idos.cz
schedule and ticket prices for public transportation (English version available)

www.berlitzpublishing.com
Berlitz Publishing website

www.cd.cz
official site of Czech Railways (English version available)

www.czechairlines.com
official site of Czech Airlines

www.caa.co.uk
U.K. Civil Aviation Authority (CAA)

www.tsa.gov
U.S. Transportation Security Administration (TSA)

English–Czech Dictionary

A

about (approximately) asi
abroad v zahraničí
accept autorizovat
accident (road) nehoda
accidentally neúmyslně
accompany doprovodit
accountant účetní
across přes
adapter adaptér
address adresa
admission charge vstupné
adult n dospělý
afraid adj vylekaný
after (time) po; **(place)** za
afternoon odpoledne
aftershave voda po holení
after-sun lotion olej po opalování
age věk
ago před
agree souhlasit
air n povětří
air conditioning klimatizace
air mattress nafukovací matrace
airline aerolinka
airmail letecká pošta
airport letiště
air-sickness letadlová nemoc
aisle seat místo u uličky

alarm clock budík
alcoholic (drink) alkoholický
all všichni
allergic alergický
allergy alergie
allowance povolené zboží
almost skoro
alone sám
already už
also také
alter upravit
aluminium foil alobal
always vždy
amazing obdivuhodný
ambassador velvyslanec
ambulance sanitka
American adj americký; n Američan
amount (money) částka
amusement park lunapark
and a
animal zvíře
another jiný
antibiotic antibiotik
antifreeze nemrznoucí směs
antique n starožitnost
any jakýkoliv
anyone někdo
apartment byt
apologize omlouvat
appendix slepé střevo
appetite chuť k jídlu
appointment setkání
approximately přibližně
area code směrové číslo

---

adj adjective   **adv** adverb   **BE** British English   **n** noun   **v** verb

architect architekt
arm paže
around (place) po; **(time)** kolem
arrive (car, train) přijet; **(plane)** přiletět
art gallery galerie
arthritis artritid
ashtray popelník
ask (question) ptát; **(request)** prosit
aspirin aspirin
asthma astma
at (place) u; **(time)** v
athletics atletika
ATM bankomat
attack útok
attractive přitažlivý
audio guide audio průvodce
aunt teta
Australia Austrálie
authentic pravý
authenticity pravost
available (free) volný

B

baby dítě
baby bottle dětská láhev
baby food kojenecká výživa
baby wipe navlhčené ubrousek
babysitter paní na hlídání děti
back (head) vzadu; **(body)** záda
backache bolest zad
backpack ruksak
bad špatný
bag kabelka

baggage [BE] zavazadlo
baggage reclaim [BE] výdej zavazadel
bakery pekařství
balcony balkón
ball míč
ballet balet
band (musical group) skupina
bandage obinadlo
bank banka
bar bar
barber holičství
basement suterén
basket košík
basketball košíková
bath n vana; v koupat
bathroom koupelna; **(toilet)** záchod
battery baterie; **(car)** akumulátor
battle site bitevní pole
be být
beach pláž
beam (headlight) světlo
beautiful krásný
because protože
bed postel
bedding přikrývky a povlečení
bedroom ložnice
before (time) před
begin začít
beginner začátečník
behind za
belong náležet
belt pásek
berth lůžko
between (time) mezi

bib bryndáček
bicycle jízdní kolo
bicycle route cyklistická stezka
big velký
bikini bikiny
bill (restaurant) účet
binoculars dalekohled
bird pták
birthday narozeniny
bite (insect) štípnutí
bitter hořký
bizarre prapodivný
bladder močový měchýř
blanket přikrývka
bleach odbarvovací prostředek
bleed krvácet
blind roleta
blister puchýř
blocked ucpaný
blood krev
blood pressure krevní tlak
blouse blůza
blow dry vyfoukat
blue modrý
board *n* palubní
boarding card palubní vstupenka
boat trip výlet lodí
boil *n* **(ailment)** vřídek; *v* vařit
boiler kotel
bone kost
book kniha
bookstore knihkupectví
boots boty
boring nudný
born narodit se
borrow půjčit

botanical garden botanická
   zahrada
bottle láhev
bottle opener otvírač na láhve
bowel střevo
bowl miska
box krabička
boy chlapec
boyfriend milenec
bra podprsenka
bracelet náramek
brakes (bicycle, car) brzdy
break *v* rozbít
breakdown porucha
breast prso
breastfeed kojit
breathe dýchat
bridge most
bring přivést
British britský
brochure brožura
broken (damaged) rozbitý; **(body
   part)** zlomený
brooch brož
brother bratr
browse dívat se
bruise modřina
bucket kyblík
building budova
bulletin board nástěnka
burn *n* popálenina
bus autobus
bus station autobusové nádraží
bus stop autobusová zastávka
business class obchodní třída
busy něco mít

but ale
butane gas plyn
butcher řezník
button knoflík
buy koupit
by (near) u; **(time)** do
bye nashledanou

C

cafe kavárna
calendar kalendář
call (shout) přijít; **(telephone)** zavolat
camera fotoaparát
camp v tábořit
campsite kempink
can opener otvírač na plechovky
Canada Kanada
canal kanál
cancel zrušit
cancer (disease) rakovina
cap (clothing) čepice; **(dental)** korunka
car auto; **(train)** vagón
car park [BE] parkoviště
car rental půjčovna aut
carafe džbánek
card karta
careful opatrný
carpet koberec
cart vozík
case (suitcase) zavazadlo
cash n **(money)** hotovost; v proplatit; **(exchange)** vyměnit
casino kasino

castle hrad
cathedral katedrála
cave jeskyně
CD cédéčko
cell phone mobilní telefon
cemetery hřbitov
center of town centrum
ceramics keramika
certificate osvědčení
chain (necklace) řetízek
change n **(coins)** drobné; v **(money)** vyměnit; **(transportation)** přestoupit; **(reservation)** změnit; **(a baby)** přebalit dítě
changing facilities prostor na přebalování
charcoal dřevěné uhlí
charter flight speciál
cheap levný
check n šek; v kontrolovat
check in (hotel) ubytovat se
check out (hotel) uvolnit pokoj
cheers na zdraví
chemist [BE] lékárna
cheque [BE] šek
chess šachy
chest (body) prsa
child dítě
child's cot [BE] dětská postýlka
child's seat dětská sedačka
church kostel
cigar doutník
cigarette cigareta
cinema [BE] kino
claim check (luggage) zavazadlový lístek

clean adj čistý; v vyčistit
cliff útes
cling film [BE] potravinová fólie
clinic zdravotní středisko
clock hodiny
close adv (near) blízko; v zavírat
clothing store oděvy
cloudy oblačný
club (golf) golfová hůl
coast pobřeží
coat kabát
coat hanger ramínko
coatroom šatna
cockroach šváb
code (phone) směrovací číslo
coin mince
cold adj studený; (weather) chladný; n chlad
collect vyzvednout
color barva
comb hřeben
come přijít
comfortable pohodlný
commission provize
company (business) firma; (companionship) společnost
computer počítač
concert koncert
concert hall koncertní síň
concession sleva
concussion otřes mozku
conditioner (hair) kondicionér
condom kondom
conductor dirigent
confirm (reservation) potvrdit
connection (train) spojení

conscious vědomí
constant nepřetržitý
constipation zácpa
consulate konzulát
consult jít
contact v spojit se
contact lens kontaktní čočka
contagious nakažlivý
contain obsahovat
contraceptive antikoncepce
cook n (chef) kuchař; v vařit
cooker [BE] (appliance) vařič
cooking facilities kuchyňské vybavení
copper měď
copy kopie
corkscrew vývrtka
correct správný
cosmetics kosmetika
cost n cena; v stát
cottage chata
cotton bavlna
cough n kašel; v kašlat
country (nation) země
course (track, path) cesta; (medication) dávka
cover charge kuvert
cramps křeče
credit card kreditní karta
credit card number číslo kreditní karty
crib kolébka
crockery [BE] nádobí
crown (dental) korunka; (royal) koruna
cruise n zábavní plavba

crystal křišťál
cup šálek
currency měna
currency exchange office
  směnárna
customs celní prohlídka
cut (hair) ostříhat
cut glass broušené sklo
cutlery příbory
cycle route cyklistická stezka
cycling cyklistika
Czech *adj* český; *n* Czech
Czech Republic Česká Republika

D

delay zpoždění
delicatessen lahůdky
delicious chutný
deliver doručit
denim džínsovina
dental floss vlákno na čištění
  mezizubních prostorů
dentist zubař
denture protéza
deodorant deodorant
depart (train, bus) odjíždět;
  (plane) odlétat
department store obchodní dům
departure lounge odjezdová hala
deposit záloha
describe popsat
details podrobnosti
detergent prášek na praní
develop (photos) vyvolat
diabetic diabetik

diamond diamant
diaper plenka
diarrhea průjem
dice kostky
dictionary slovník
diesel (fuel) nafta; **(vehicle)**
  dieselový motor
diet dieta
difficult těžký
digital camera digitální fotoaparát
dining car jídelní vůz
dining room jídelna
dinner večeře
direct (train, flight) přímý
direction směr
directory (telephone) telefonní
  seznam
dirty špinavý
disabled *adj* tělesně postižený;
  n invalida
discount sleva
dish (meal) jídlo; **(tableware)**
  nádoba
dishcloth hadr na nádobí
dishwashing liquid prostředek na
  mytí nádobí
display window vitrína
disposable camera fotoaparát na
  jedno použití
dive skákat do vody
divorced rozvedený
dizzy závrativý
doctor doktor
doll panenka
dollar (U.S.) dolar
door dveře

double bed manželská postel
downtown centrum města
dozen tucet
dress šaty
drink *n* pití; *v* pít
drive jet
driver řidič
driver's license řidičský průkaz
drowning topit se
drugstore drogerie
dry clean *v* chemicky vyčistit
dry cleaner čistírna
dubbed dabovaný
dummy [BE] dudlík
during během
dustbin [BE] popelnica
duvet peřina
ear ucho

E

ear drops kapky do uší
early brzo
earring náušnice
east východ
easy snadný
eat jíst
economy class ekonomická třída
elastic *adj* elastický
electric razor elektrický holicí strojek
electrical outlet elektrické zásuvka
electronic elektronický
elevator výtah
e-mail elektronická pošta
e-mail address emailová adresa

embassy velvyslanectví
emerald smaragd
emergency *adj* naléhavý
emergency exit nouzový východ
empty prázdný
enamel email
end končit
engaged zasnoubený
engine motor
engineering strojírenství
England Anglie
English *adj* anglický; **(language)** angličtina; *n* Anglik
enjoy mít rád
enlarge zvětšit
enough dost
entertainment guide kulturní přehled
entrance fee vstupné
entry visa vstupní vízum
envelope obálka
epileptic *n* epileptik
equipment (sports) vybavení
error chyba
escalator eskalátor
essential nezbytný
e-ticket elektronický lístek
evening večer
every každý
examination (medical) vyšetření
example příklad
except kromě
excess luggage nadváha
excursion výlet
exhausted vyčerpaný
exchange *v* vyměnit

exchange rate kurz
exit *n* východ; **(highway)** sjezd
expensive drahý
exposure (photos) snímek
express spěšně
extension linka
extract (tooth) vytrhnout

F

fabric látka
face obličej
facial ošetřit obličej
facility zručnost
factor (sunscreen) faktor
family rodina
famous známý
fan (ventilation) větrák
far daleko sighted
farm statek
far-sighted dalekozraký
fast (clock) rychlý napřed
fast-food restaurant rychlé
    občerstvení
father otec
faucet kohoutek
faulty vadné
favorite oblíbený
fax fax
feed nakojit
feel cítit
female *adj* ženská; *n* žena
fever horečka
few málo
field pole
fight (brawl) rvačka

fill vyplnit
filling (dental) plomba
film (movie) film; **(camera)** film
filter filtr
find najít
fine (well) dobře; **(penalty)** pokuta
finger prst
fire krb; **(disaster)** požár
fire alarm požární hlásič
fire brigade [BE] hasiči
fire department hasiči
fire exit nouzový východ
fire extinguisher hasicí přístroj
first class první třída
fit (clothes) slušet
fitting room zkušební kabina
fix spravit
flashlight ruční
flat (puncture) píchlý
flavor příchuť
flea blecha
flight letadlo
flight number let číslo
floor (level) poschodí
florist květiny
flower květ
flu (influenza) chřipka
fly (insect) moucha
foggy mlhavo
food jídlo
food poisoning otrava potravinami
foot chodidlo
football [BE] fotbal
footpath pěšina
for (time) na; **(towards)** do
foreign currency zahraniční měna

forest les
forget zapomenout
fork vidlička
form formulář
formal dress formální oblečení
fortunately naštěstí
fountain kašna
foyer (hotel, theater) foyer
fracture zlomenina
frame (glasses) obroučky
free (available) volný; (no charge) zadarmo
freezer mraznička
frequent často
fresh čerstvý
friend přítel
friendly přátelský
frightened vystrašený
from (place) z; (time) od
front adj přední; (head) vpředu
frost mráz
frying pan pánev
fuel palivo
full (filled) plný; (after meal) obsazený
fun zábava
furniture nábytek
fuse pojistka

G

game (sport) zápas; (toy) hra
garage (parking) garáž; (repair) servis
garbage bag pytel na odpadky
garden zahrada

gas benzín
gas station benzínová pumpa
gate (airport) východ
gauze gáza
genuine originál
gift dárek
girl děvče
girlfriend milenka
give dát
gland žláza
glass (drinking) sklenice
glasses (optical) brýle
glove rukavice
go (on foot) jít; (by vehicle) jet
goggles potápěčské brýle
gold zlato
golf golf
golf course golfové hřiště
good dobrý; (delicious) výborný
grandparents prarodiče
grass tráva
gray šedý
great úžasný
green zelený
greengrocer [BE] ovoce a zelenina
grocery store potraviny
ground (earth) zem
ground floor [BE] přízemí
groundcloth [BE] podlážka
groundsheet podlážka
group skupina
guarantee záruka
guest house penzión
guide průvodce
guided tour prohlídka s průvodcem
guided walk vycházka s průvodcem

guitar kytara
gynecologist gynekolog

H

hair vlasy
hairdresser kadeřník
hairdryer fén
hairspray lak na vlasy
half půl
hammer kladivo
hand (body) ruka
handbag kabelka
handicapped *adj* tělesně postižený
handicrafts řemesla
handkerchief kapesník
hand-washable prát v ruce
hanger ramínko
hangover *n* kocovina
happen stát se
harbor přístav
hard (firm) tvrdý; **(difficult)** obtížný
hat klobouk
have mít
hay fever senná rýma
head hlava
health zdraví
health food store zdravá výživa
health insurance zdravotní pojištění
hear slyšet
hearing aid sluchadlo
heart *n* srdce; **(cards)** srdce
heart attack infarkt
heat topení
heavy těžký
height výška

hemorrhoids hemoroidy
here (motion) sem; **(place)** tady
hernia kýla
high vysoký
highway dálnice
hiking *n* pěší turistika
hiking gear vybavení na turistiku
hill kopec
hire půjčit
historic site památková oblast
hobby (pastime) koníček
hold (wait) počkat
hole díra
holiday [BE] dovolená
holiday resort [BE] rekreační středisko
home domů
honeymoon svatebná cestě
hopefully snad
horse kůň
horse racing dostihy
hospital nemocnice
hot (temperature) horký; **(weather)** horko
hotel hotel
hour hodin
house dům
how jak
hundred sto
hunger hlad
hungry hladový
hurt bolet
husband manžel

I

ice led
icy zledovatělý
identification identifikace
ill nemocný
illegal nezákonné
imitation napodobenina
in (place) v; (within a period of time) za
include zahrnovat
incredible neuvěřitelný
indicate ukázat
indigestion porucha trávení
indoor pool krytý bazén
inexpensive levný
infection infekce
inflammation zánět
informal (dress) neformální
information informace
information office turistická kancelář
injection injekce
innocent nevinný
insect hmyz
insect bite štípanec
insect repellent repelent proti hmyzu
inside uvnitř
insomnia nespavost
instead místo
instructions návod
instructor instruktor
insulin inzulín
insurance (car) pojištění; (company) pojišťovna
insurance card pojistka

insurance certificate [BE] pojistka
insurance claim pojistná škoda
interest (hobby) zájem
interesting zajímavý
International Student Card mezinárodní studentský průkaz
internet internet
internet cafe internetová kavárna
interpreter tlumočník
intersection křižovatka
into do
invite pozvat
iodine jód
Ireland Irsko
item předmět
itemized bill rozepsaný účet
itch svědět

J

jacket sako
jaw čelist
jazz džez
jeans džíny
jet lag časový posun
jeweler klenoty mpl
job práce
join přidat
joint kloub
joke vtip
journalist novinář
journey cesta
jug (water) džbánek
junction křižovatka

K

keep nechat si
kerosene petrolej
kettle konvice
key klíč m
key card kličevá karta
key ring přívěsek ke klíčům
kiddie pool dětský bazén
kidney ledvina
kilometer kilometr
kind (pleasant) hodný
kiss n políbení; v políbit
kitchen kuchyně
kitchen foil [BE] alobal
knee koleno
knife nůž
know znát
kosher košer

L

label nálepka
lace krajka
ladder žebřík
lake jezero
lamp lampa
land (airplane) přistát
language course jazykový kurz
large velký
last adj poslední; v vydržet
late pozdě
laundromat prádelna
laundry facilities prádelna
lavatory záchod
lawyer právník

laxative projímadlo
lead v vést
leak n prosakování; v (roof, pipe) téct
learn učit se
leather kůže
leave (aircraft) odlétat; (by vehicle) odjíždět; (on foot) odejít
left vlevo
left-luggage office [BE] úschovna zavazadel
leg noha
legal legální
lend půjčit
length délka
lens (camera) čočka
lens cap víčko na čočku
less méně
lesson hodina
letter dopis
level adj rovný
library knihovna
life život
life boat záchranný člun
life jacket záchranná vesta
lifeguard plavčík jacket
lift [BE] výtah; (hitchhiking) svezení
lift pass permanentka na vlek
light (color) světlý; (weight) lehký; (electric) světlo
lightbulb žárovka
lighter (cigarette) zapalovač
like líbit; (want) chtít; (activities) mít rád
line (subway) trasa
linen len

lip ret
lipstick rtěnka
liquor store obchod lihovinami
liter litr
little (small) malý
live žít
liver játra
living room obývací pokoj
lobby (theater, hotel) vestibul
local místní
lock n zámek; v zamknout
log on zalogovat
long dlouhý
long-distance bus dálkový autobus
long-sighted [BE] dalekozraký
look hledat
loose volný
lorry [BE] nákladní auto
lose ztratit
lost property office [BE] ztráty
    a nálezy
lost-and-found ztráty a nálezy
lot hodně
loud hlasitý
love milovat
lovely krásně
low nízký
luck štěstí
luggage zavazadla
luggage cart vozík na zavazadla
luggage trolley [BE] vozík na
    zavazadla
lump boule
lung plíce
lunch oběd

M

madam paní
magazine časopis
magnificent velkolepý
machine washable prát v pračce
maid (hotel) pokojská; **(home)**
    služebná
mail n pošta; v poslat
mailbox poštovní schránka
main hlavní
make-up make·up
male adj mužský; n muž
mallet palice
man pán
manager vedoucí
manicure manikúra
manual (car) manuální
many mnoho
map mapa
market tržnice
married (man) ženatý; **(woman)**
    vdaná
mascara řasenka
mask (diving) potápěčská maska
mass mše
massage masáž
match (game) zápas
matches zápalky
mattress matrace
maybe možná
mean v mínit
measure změřit
measurement míra
medication lék
medicine lék

medium (size) střední
meet setkat se
mechanic mechanik
member člen
menu jídelní lístek
message vzkaz
metal kov
microwave (oven) mikrovlnná trouba
midday [BE] poledne
midnight půlnoc
migraine migréna
million milión
mini-bar minibar
minute minuta
mirror zrcadlo
missing chybět
mistake (error) chyba;
    (misunderstanding) omyl
mobile phone [BE] mobilní telefon
moisturizer (cream) zvlhčující
    krém
monastery klášter
money peníze
money order poštovní poukázka
month měsíc
moped moped
more více
mosque mešita
mosquito bite štípnutí komárem
mother matka
motion sickness cestovní nemoc
motor boat motorový člun
motorcycle motocykl
motorway [BE] dálnice
mountain hora
mountain bike horské kolo

mountain pass horský průsmyk
mountain range horské pásmo
mouth ústa
movie film
movie theater kino
mugging přepadení
much hodně
muscle sval
museum muzeum
music hudba
musician hudebník

N

name jméno
napkin ubrousek
nappy [BE] plenka
narrow úzký
national národní
nationality státní příslušnost
nature přirozenost
nature reserve přírodní rezervace
nausea žaludeční nevolnost
near blízko
near-sighted krátkozraký
necessary nutný
neck (head) krk
necklace náhrdelník
need *n* nutnost; *v* potřebovat
nerve nerv
nervous system nervový systém
never nikdy
new nový
New Zealand Nový Zéland
newspaper noviny
newsstand novinový stánek

next (in a row) další; **(in a row)** nejbližší; **(in time)** příští
nice hezký
night noc
night club noční klub
noisy hlučný
non-alcoholic nealkoholický
none žádný
non-smoking nekuřáci
noon poledne
normal běžný
north sever
nose nos
nothing nic
notify uvědomit
now nyní
number číslo
nurse zdravotní sestra
nylon nylon

O

occasionally občas
occupied obsazený
office kancelář
off-licence [BE] obchod lihovinami
off-peak mimo špičku
often často
oil olej
old starý
old town staré město
on v
once jednou
one-way ticket (train) jízdenka jedním směrem; **(plane)** letenka jedním směrem

open *adj* otevřený; *v* otvírat
opening hours otevírací doba
opera opera
opera house operní divadlo
operation (medical) operace
opposite naproti
optician optik
or nebo
orange (color) oranžový
order objednat
organized organizovaný
orchestra orchestr
outdoor venkovní
outdoor pool venkovní bazén
outrageous nestydatý
outside venku
oval oválný
oven trouba
overheat přehřátí
overnight přes noc
owe dlužit
own *v* vlastnit

P

pacifier dudlík
pack balit
package balík
paddling pool [BE] dětský bazén
padlock visací zámek
pail kyblík
pain bolest
painkiller lék proti bolesti
paint malovat
painting malířství obraz
palace palác

palpitations bušení srdce
panorama panoráma
pants kalhoty
panty hose punčochové kalhoty
paralysis ochrnutí
parcel [BE] balík
parents rodiče
park park
parking lot parkoviště
parking meter parkovací hodiny
parliament building budova parlamentu
partner (male) partner; **(female)** partnerka
party (social) společnost; **(event)** večírek
passport pas
pastry shop cukrárna
patch v spravit
patient n pacient
pavement chodník
pay zaplatit
pay phone telefonní budka
payment platba
peak vrchol
pearl perla
pedestrian pěšák
pedestrian crossing přechod pro chodce
pedestrian precinct [BE] pěší zóna
pedestrian zone pěší zóna
pen pero
people lidé
perhaps možná
period (menstrual) menstruace
petrol [BE] benzín

petrol station [BE] benzínová pumpa
pewter cín
pharmacy lékárna
phone v telefonovat
phone card telefonní karta
photo vyfotografovat
photo fotografie
photocopier kopírka
phrase věta
phrase book konverzační příručka
pick up (something) vyzvednout si
picnic piknik
picnic area místo na piknik
piece kousek
pill tableta; **(contraceptive)** antikoncepční pilulka
pillow polštář
pillow case povlak na polštář
pilot light plamínek
pink růžový
pipe (smoking) dýmka
plan plán
plane letadlo
plant n rostlina
plaster [BE] náplast
plastic bag igelitová taška
plate talíř
platform nástupiště
platinum platina
play n představení; v hrát
playground dětské hřiště
pleasant příjemný
please prosím
plug zástrčka
pneumonia zápal plic

point *v* ukázat
poison jed
police policie report
police report zpráva od policie
police station policejní stanice
pollen count hladina pylu
polyester polyester
pond rybník
popular populární
port (harbor) přístav
porter nosič
portion porce
post [BE] *n* pošta; *v* podat na poště
postbox [BE] poštovní schránka
postcard pohlednice
pottery keramika
pound (sterling) libra
power energie
pregnant těhotná
prescribe předepsat
prescription předpis
present (gift) dárek
press vyžehlit
pretty hezký
price cena
prison vězení
profession povolání
program program
pronounce vyslovit
pub hospoda
public *n* veřejnost
pump (gas station) pumpa
puncture píchlý
pure čistý
purse kabelka
pushchair [BE] kočárek

Q

quality *adj* kvalitní
quarter čtvrt
queue [BE] *n* fronta; *v* stát ve frontě
quick rychlý
quiet tichý

R

racetrack závodní dráha
racket (tennis, squash) raketa
railway [BE] železnice
railway station [BE] nádraží
rain *n* déšť; *v* pršet
raincoat pláštěnka
rape znásilnění
rapids peřej
rash vyrážka
razor holicí strojek
ready hotový
real (genuine) pravý
rear zadní
receipt (payment) stvrzenka
reception (desk) recepce
receptionist recepční
recommend doporučit
reduction (in price) sleva
refrigerator lednice
refund *n* náhrada; *v* vrátit peníze
region (geographical) oblast
registered mail doporučeně
registration form registrační karta
regular obyčejný
reliable spolehlivý
religion vyznání

rent půjčit
rental car auto z půjčovny
repair v opravit
repeat zopakovat
replacement adj náhradní
replacement part náhradní díl
report (crime) ohlásit
require potřebovat
required (necessary) nutný
reservation rezervace; **(on a train)** místenka
reserve zamluvit
rest v odpočívat
restaurant restaurace
retired v důchodu
return vrátit se; **(give back)** vrátit
return ticket [BE] (train) zpáteční jízdenka; **(plane)** zpáteční letenka
rheumatism revmatismus
rib žebro
right správný
right of way (in a car) přednost; **(access)** přístupný
ring prsten
river řeka
road silnice
road map automapa
robbery loupež
romantic romantický
roof (house, car) střecha
room pokoj
rope lano
round kulatý
round-trip ticket zpáteční lístek
route cesta

rude nezdvořilý
ruins zříceniny
rush hour špička

S

safe adj **(not dangerous)** bezpečný; **(feeling)** bezpečně; n sejf
safety bezpečí
sales tax DPH
same stejný
sand písek
sandals sandály
sanitary napkin dámská vložka
sanitary pad [BE] dámská vložka
satin satén
satisfied spokojený
sauna sauna
scarf šátek
scissors nůžky
Scotland Skotsko
screwdriver šroubovák
sea moře
seasickness mořskou nemoc
season ticket sezónní lístek
seat (on train, etc.) místo; **(theater)** sedadlo
second class druhá třída
secretary sekretářka
sedative sedativum
see vidět; **(inspect)** podívat se
self-employed soukromník
self-service (gas station) samoobsluha
sell prodávat
send poslat

senior citizen starší občan
separately samostatně
serious závažný
service (in restaurant) obsluha;
  (religious) bohoslužba
shade odstín
shallow mělký
shampoo šampon
share rozdělovat se
sharp ostrý
shaving cream krém na holení
sheet (bed) povlečení
shirt (men's) košile
shock (electric) šok
shoe bot
shoe store obchod s obuví
shopping area oblast s obchody
shopping basket nákupní košík
shopping centre [BE] obchodní
  centrum
shopping mall obchodní centrum
short (opp. long) krátký; **(opp. tall)**
  nízký; **(height)** malý
shorts krátké kalhoty
short-sighted [BE] krátkozraký
shoulder rameno
shovel lopatka
show ukázat
shower sprcha
shut *adj* zavřený; *v* zavírat
sights pamětihodnosti
sightseeing tour prohlídka
sign (road sign) značka
signpost [BE] ukazatel
silk hedvábí
silver stříbro

singer zpěvák
single (unmarried) svobodný
single room jednolůžkový pokoj
single ticket [BE] (train) jízdenka
  jedním směrem; **(plane)** letenka
  jedním směrem
sink umyvadlo
sister sestra
sit sedět
size velikost
skates brusle
ski *n* lyže; *v* lyžovat
ski boots lyžařské boty
ski poles lyžařské hole
skin pokožka
skirt sukně
sleep spát
sleeping bag spací pytel
sleeping car lůžkový vůz
sleeping pill prášek na spaní
sleeve rukáv
slice plátek
slippers papuče
slow pomalý
small malý
small change drobné
smell zápach
smoke *v* zapálit
smoking kuřáci
sneakers tenisky
snorkel šnorchl
snow *n* sníh; *v* sněžit
soap mýdlo
soccer fotbal
socket zástrčka
socks ponožky

something něco
sometimes někdy
son syn
soon brzo
sore bolí
sour kyselý
south jih
souvenir suvenýr
space místo
spare (part) náhradní; **(extra)** navíc
speak mluvit
special zvláštní
specialist specialista
specimen vzorek
spell hláskovat
spend (time, money) strávit;
  (waste) utratit
spicy kořeněný
sponge houba
spoon lžíce
sport sport
sporting goods store sportovní
  potřeby
sports club sportovní klub
spot (place, site) místo
sprained vyvrtnutý
square náměstí
stadium stadion
staff personál
stain skvrna
stairs schodiště
stamp známka
stand stát
standby ticket lístek na čekací
  listině
start začínat

statement (police) prohlášení
stationery store papírnictví
statue socha
stay (remain) zůstat
steal ukrást
sterilizing solution sterilizační
  roztok
stockings punčochy
stolen adj ukradený
stomach žaludek
stomachache bolení břicha
stop (bus) stanice; v stavět
store guide informační tabule
stormy bouřka
stove vařič
strange divný
straw brčko
stream potok
stroller kočárek
strong silný
student student
study studovat
style styl
subtitled s titulky
subway metro
subway map plán metra
subway station stanice metra
suggest doporučit
suit (man's) oblek; **(woman's)**
  kostým
suitable vhodný
summer léto
sun slunce
sunbathe opalovat se
sunglasses sluneční brýle
sunstroke úžeh

superb skvělý
supermarket samoobsluha
supervision dozor
supplement přirážka
suppository čípek
sure určitě
surname příjmení
sweater svetr
sweatshirt tričko
sweet (taste) sladký
swelling oteklina
swim suit
swimming pool bazén
swimming trunks pánské plavky
swimsuit dámské plavky
swollen oteklý
symptom (illness) příznak
synagogue synagoga
synthetic umělý

T

table stůl
take (medicine) užívat; **(carry)** vzít
talk mluvit
tall vysoký
tampon tampón
tan opálení
taxi taxík
taxi rank [BE] stanoviště taxíků
taxi stand stanoviště taxíků
teacher učitel
team tým
teddy bear medvídek
telephone *n* telefon; *v* zatelefonovat
telephone bill účet za telefon

telephone booth telefonní budka
telephone call telefonický hovor
telephone number telefonní číslo
temperature (body) teplota
temple chrám
temporarily dočasně
tennis tenis
tennis court tenisový kurt
tent stan
tent pegs stanové kolíčky
terrace terasa
terrible hrozný
terrific báječně
theater divadlo
theft krádež
then (time) potom
there tam
thermometer teploměr
thermos termoska
thick silný
thief zloděj
thigh stehno
thin (not thick) slabý; **(narrow)**
tenký; **(weight)** hubený
thirsty žíznivý
throat krk
through přes
thumb palec
ticket (train) jízdenka; **(plane)**
letenka; **(theater, etc.)** lístek
ticket office pokladna
tie kravata
tight těsný
tights punčochové kalhoty
tin opener [BE] otvírač na
plechovky

tired unavený
tissue papírový kapesník
to (place, purpose) k
tobacco tabák
tobacconist tabák
today dnes
toe prst na noze
toilet záchod
toilet paper toaletní papír
tomorrow zítra
tongue jazyk
tonight dnes večer
too (extreme) moc
tooth zub
toothbrush kartáček na zuby
toothpaste zubní pasta
torch ruční svítilna
torn natržený
tough (food) tuhý
tour zájezd
tour guide průvodce
tourist turista
tourist office turistická kancelář
tow truck havarijní služba
towel ručník
tower věž
town město
town hall radnice
toy hračka
traditional tradiční
traffic doprava
traffic jam dopravní zácpa
traffic offence [BE] dopravní
    přestupek
traffic violation dopravní přestupek
trailer obytný přívěs

train vlak
train station nádraží
tram tramvaj
transit *v* projíždět
translate přeložit
translation překlad
translator překladatel
travel agency cestovní kancelář
travel sickness cestovní nemoc
travelers check cestovní šek
travellers cheque [BE] cestovní šek
tray podnos
tree strom
trim zastřihnout
trip cesta
trolley vozík
trousers [BE] kalhoty
truck nákladní automobil
T-shirt triko
tumor nádor
tunnel tunel
turn down (volume) stáhnout
turn off vypnout
turn on zapnout
turn up (volume) zesílit
TV televize
tweezers pinzeta
type *n* typ
typical typický

U

ugly ošklivý
ulcer vřed
umbrella (sun) slunečník; **(rain)**
    deštník

uncle strýc
under pod
underground [BE] metro
underground station [BE] stanice metra
understand rozumět
underwear spodní prádlo
undress svléknout se
uneven (ground) hrbolatý
unfortunately bohužel
uniform uniforma
unit (for a phone card) jednotka
United Kingdom Velké Británie
United States Spojené Státy
unleaded (gas) bezolovnatý
unlimited mileage počet kilometrů není omezen
unlock odemknout
unpleasant nepříjemný
unscrew odšroubovat
until do
upper (berth) nahoře
upset stomach bolení břicha
urine moč
use n potřeba; v použít
utensils příbory

V

vacant volný
vacation dovolená
vaginal infection vaginální infekce
valet service parkovací služby
valid platný
validate (tickets) potvrdit
valley údolí

valuable cenný
valve uzavírací kohout
VAT [BE] DPH
VAT receipt [BE] daň z přidané hodnoty
vegetarian vegetariánský
vein žíla
venereal disease pohlavní nemoc
ventilator větrák
very velmi
video game video hra
viewpoint vyhlídka
village vesnice
vineyard vinice
visa vízum
visit v navštívit; (see sights) podívat se
visiting hours návštěvní hodiny
volleyball volejbal
voltage napětí
vomit zvracet

W

wait počkat
waiter vrchní
waiting room čekárna
wake vzbudit
wake-up call buzení telefonem
walking route turistická cesta
wallet peněženka
war memorial památník obětem války
ward (hospital) oddělení
warm teplý
washing machine pračka

wasp vosa
water voda
waterfall vodopád
waterproof vodotěsný
waterproof jacket nepromokavá bunda
watch *n* hodinky
wave vlna
wear mít na sobě
weather počasí
weather forecast předpověď počasí
wedding svatba
week týden
weekend víkend
weekend rate víkendová sazba
west západ
wet mokrý
wetsuit neoprenový oblek
wheelchair kolečková židle
when kdy
where kde
which který
who kdo
whose čí
wide široký
wife manželka
wildlife divoká příroda
wind vítr
window okno; **(store)** výloha
window seat sedadlo u okna
wireless internet bezdrátový internet
with s
withdraw vyzvednout
within (time) do
without bez

witness svědek
wood les
wool vlna
work (function) fungovat
worse horší
write napsat
wrong chybný

X

x-ray rentgen

Y

yacht jachta
year rok
yes ano
yesterday včera
young mladý
youth hostel mládežnická ubytovna

Z

zero nula
zipper zip
zoo zoo

Czech–English Dictionary

A

a and
adaptér adapter
adresa address
aerolinka airline
akumulátor battery (car)
ale but
alergický allergic
alergie allergy
alkoholický alcoholic (drink)
alobal aluminum [kitchen BE] foil
americký *adj* American
Američan *n* American
anestetický anesthetic
anestetikum anasthetia
anglický *adj* English
angličtina English (language)
Anglie England
Anglik *n* English
ano yes
antibiotik antibiotic
antikoncepce contraceptive
antikoncepční pilulka pill
  (contraceptive)
architekt architect
artritid arthritis
asi about (approximately)
aspirin aspirin
astma asthma
atletika athletics
audio průvodce audio guide

Austrálie Australia
auto car
auto z půjčovny rental car
autobus bus
autobusová zastávka bus stop
autobusové nádraží bus station
automapa road map
autorizovat accept
až k up to

B

báječně terrific
balet ballet
balík package
balit pack
balkón balcony
banka bank
bankomat ATM
bar bar
barva color
baterie battery
bavlna cotton
bazén swimming pool
během during
benzín gas [petrol BE]
benzínová pumpa gas [petrol BE]
  station
bez without
bezolovnatý unleaded
bezpečí safety
bezpečně *adv* safe (feeling)
bezpečný *adj* safe (not dangerous)
běžný normal
bikiny bikini
bitevní pole battle site

blecha flea
blízko *adv* close (near)
blůza blouse
bohoslužba service (religious)
bohužel unfortunately
bolení břicha stomachache
bolest pain
bolest zad backache
bolet hurt
bolí sore
bot shoe
botanická zahrada botanical garden
boty boots
boule lump
bouřka stormy
bratr brother
brčko straw
britský British
broušené sklo cut glass
brož brooch
brožura brochure
brusle skates
brýle glasses (optical)
bryndáček bib
brzdy brakes (car, bicycle)
brzo soon
budík alarm clock
budova building
budova parlamentu parliament building
budovat built
bušení srdce palpitations
buzení telefonem wake-up call
byt apartment
být be

C

cédéčko CD
celní prohlídka customs
cena *n* cost; price
cenný valuable
centrum center of town
centrum města downtown
cesta course (track, path); route; trip
cestovní kancelář travel agency
cestovní nemoc motion sickness
cestovní šek travelers check [cheque BE]
cigareta cigarette
cín pewter
cítit feel
cukrárna pastry shop
cyklistická stezka cycle route
cyklistika cycling
Czech *n* Czech

Č

časopis magazine
časový posun jet lag
částka amount (money)
často *adv* often
čekárna waiting room
čelist jaw
čepice cap (clothing)
čerstvý fresh
Česká Republika Czech Republic
český *adj* Czech
čí whose
čípek suppository
číslo number

číslo kreditní karty credit card number
čistírna dry cleaner
čistý *adj* clean, pure
člen member
čočka lens (camera)
čtrnáct dní fortnight
čtvrt quarter

D

dabovaný dubbed
dalekohled binoculars
dalekozraký far-sighted [long-sighted BE]
dálkový autobus long-distance bus
dálnice highway [motorway BE]
další next (subsequent)
dámská vložka sanitary napkin [pad BE]
dámské plavky swimsuit
dárek gift
dát give
dávka course (medication)
dcera daughter
délka length
den day
denně daily
denní jízdenka day ticket
deodorant deodorant
destilovaná voda distilled water
déšť *n* rain
deštník umbrella (rain)
dětská láhev baby bottle
dětská postýlka crib [child's cot BE]
dětská sedačka child's seat

dětské hřiště playground
dětský bazén kiddie [paddling BE] pool
děvče girl
diabetik diabetic
diamant diamond
dieselový motor diesel (vehicle)
dieta diet
digitální fotoaparát digital camera
díra hole
dirigent conductor
diskotéka dance club
dítě child; baby
divadlo theater
dívat se browse
divný strange
divoká příroda wildlife
dlouhý long
dlužit owe
dnes today
dnes večer tonight
do by (time); for (towards); into; until
dobrý good
dobře fine (well)
dočasně temporarily
doktor doctor
dolar dollar (U.S.)
domů home
dopis letter
doporučeně registered mail
doporučit recommend
doprava traffic
dopravní přestupek traffic violation [offence BE]
dopravní zácpa traffic jam
doprovodit accompany

doručit deliver
dospělý *n* adult
dost enough
dostihová dráha race track
dostihy horse racing
doutník cigar
dovolená vacation [holiday BE]
dozor supervision
DPH sales tax [VAT BE]
drahý expensive
drobné *n* change (coins)
drogerie drugstore
druhá třída second class
dřevěné uhlí charcoal
dudlík pacifier [dummy BE]
dům house
dvě lůžka twin beds
dveře door
dýchat breathe
dýmka pipe (smoking)
džbánek carafe; jug (water)
džez jazz
džínsovina denim
džíny jeans

emailová adresa e-mail address
energie power
epileptik *n* epileptic
eskalátor escalator

hasiči fire department [brigade BE]
havarijní služba tow truck
hedvábí silk
hemoroidy hemorrhoids
hezký nice; pretty
hlad hunger
hladina pylu pollen count
hladový hungry
hlasitý loud
hláskovat spell
hlava head
hlavní main
hledat look
hluboký deep
hlučný noisy
hluchý deaf
hmyz insect
hodin hour
hodina lesson
hodinky n watch
hodiny clock
hodně much
hodný kind (pleasant)
holčička girl (little girl)
holicí strojek razor
holičství barber
hora mountain
horečka fever
horko adv hot (weather)
horký adj hot (temperature)
horské kolo mountain bike
horské pásmo mountain range
horský průsmyk mountain pass
horší worse
hořký bitter
hospoda pub

hotel hotel
hotovost cash (money)
hotový ready
houba sponge
hra game (toy)
hračka toy
hrad castle
hrát v play
hrbolatý uneven (ground)
hrozný terrible
hřbitov cemetery
hřeben comb
hubený thin (weight)
hudba music
hudebník musician

CH

chata cottage
chemicky vyčistit v dry clean
chlad n cold
chladný cold (weather)
chlapec boy
chodidlo foot
chodník pavement
chrám temple
chřipka flu (influenza)
chtít like (want)
chuť k jídlu appetite
chutný delicious
chyba error
chyba mistake (error)
chybět missing
chybný wrong

identifikace identification
igelitová taška plastic bag
infarkt heart attack
infekce infection
informace information
informační tabule store guide
injekce injection
instruktor instructor
internet internet
internetová kavárna internet cafe
invalida *n* disabled
inzulín insulin
Irsko Ireland

jezero lake
jídelna dining room
jídelní lístek menu
jídelní vůz dining car
jídlo food
jih south
jiný another
jíst eat
jít go (on foot)
jízdenka ticket (train)
jízdenka jedním směrem one-way
[single BE] ticket (train)
jízdní kolo bicycle
jméno name
jód iodine

jachta yacht
jak how
jakýkoliv any
jaro spring
játra liver
jazyk tongue
jazykový kurz language course
jed poison
jedním směrem one-way (ticket)
jednodenní výlet day trip
jednolůžkový pokoj single room
jednotka unit (for a phone card)
jednou once
jeho his
její her(s)
jejich their(s)
jeskyně cave
jet drive

k to (place, purpose)
kabát coat
kadeřnictví hairdresser
kalendář calendar
kalhoty pants [trousers BE]
kamaše leggings
Kanada Canada
kanál canal
kancelář office
kapesník handkerchief
kapky do uší ear drops
karta card
kartáček na zuby toothbrush
kasino casino
kašel *n* cough
kašlat *v* cough
kašna fountain
katedrála cathedral

kavárna café
každý every
kde where
kdo who
kdy when
kempink campsite
keramika pottery
kilometr kilometer
kino movie theater [cinema BE]
kladivo hammer
klášter monastery
klenotník jeweler
klíč key
kličevá karta key card
klimatizace air conditioning
klobouk hat
kloub joint
kniha book
knihkupectví bookstore
knihovna library
knír moustache
knoflík button
koberec carpet
kocovina *n* hangover
kočárek stroller [pushchair BE]
kojenecká výživa baby food
kojit breastfeed
kolečková židle wheelchair
kolem around (time)
koleno knee
koncert concert
koncertní síň concert hall
končit end
kondicionér conditioner (hair)
kondom condom
koníček hobby (pastime)

kontaktní čočka contact lens
kontrolovat *v* check
konverzační příručka phrase book
konvice kettle
konzulát consulate
kopec hill
kopie copy
kopírka photocopier
koruna crown (royal; Czech currency)
korunka crown (dental)
kořeněný spicy
kosmetika cosmetics
kost bone
kostel church
kostky dice
kostým suit (woman's)
košer kosher
košík basket
košíková basketball
košile shirt (men's)
kotel boiler
koupat *v* bath
koupelna bathroom
koupit buy
kousek piece
kov metal
krabička box
krádež theft
krajka lace
krásně *adv* lovely
krásný *adj* beautiful
krátké kalhoty shorts
krátkozraký near-sighted [short-sighted BE]
krátký short (not long)

kravata tie
krb fire
kreditní karta credit card
krém na holení shaving cream
krev blood
krevní tlak blood pressure
krk neck; throat
kromě except
krvácet bleed
krytý bazén indoor pool
křeče cramps
křišťál crystal
křižovatka intersection; junction
který which
kuchař *n* cook (chef)
kuchyňské vybavení cooking facilities
kulatý round
kulturní přehled entertainment guide
kůň horse
kurz exchange rate
kuřáci smoking
kuvert cover charge
kůže leather
kvalitní *adj* quality
květ flower
květiny florist
kyblík bucket
kýla hernia
kyselý sour
kytara guitar

láhev bottle

lahůdky delicatessen
lak na vlasy hair spray
lampa lamp
lano rope
látka fabric
led ice
lednice refrigerator
ledvina kidney
legální legal
lehký light (weight)
lék medication
lék proti bolesti painkiller
lékárna pharmacy [chemist BE]
len linen
les forest
let číslo flight number
letadlo plane
letadlová nemoc air-sickness
letecká pošta airmail
letenka ticket (plane)
letenka jedním směrem one-way [single BE] ticket (plane)
letiště airport
léto summer
levný cheap
líbit like
libra pound (sterling)
lidé people
linka extension
lístek ticket (theater)
lístek na čekací listině standby ticket
litr liter
lopatka shovel
loupež robbery
ložnice bedroom

lunapark amusement park
lůžko berth
lůžkový vůz sleeping car
lyžařské boty ski boots
lyžařské hole ski poles
lyže *n* ski
lyžovat *v* ski
lžíce spoon

M

make-up make-up
malířství obraz painting
málo few
malovat paint
malý little (small); short (height);
mandle tonsils
manikúra manicure
manuální manual (car)
manžel husband
manželka wife
manželská postel double bed
mapa map
masáž massage
matka mother
matrace mattress
měď copper
medvídek teddy bear
mechanik mechanic
mělký shallow
měna currency
méně less
menstruace period (menstrual)
měsíc month
město town
mešita mosque

mezi between (time)
mezinárodní studentský průkaz
    International Student Card
míč ball
migréna migraine
mikrovlnná trouba microwave (oven)
milenec boyfriend
milenka girlfriend
milión million
milovat love
mimo špičku off-peak
mince coin
minibar mini-bar
mínit *v* mean
minuta minute
míra measurement
miska bowl
místenka reservation (on a train)
místo instead; seat (on train); spot
    (place, site)
místo na piknik picnic area
místo u uličky aisle seat
mít have
mít na sobě wear
mít rád enjoy
mládežnická ubytovna youth hostel
mladý young
mlhavo foggy
mluvit talk; speak
mnoho many
mobilní telefon cell [mobile BE]
    phone
moč urine
močový měchýř bladder
modrý blue
modřina bruise

mokrý wet
moped moped
moře sea
mořskou nemoc seasickness
most bridge
motocykl motorcycle
motor engine
motorový člun motor boat
moucha fly (insect)
možná maybe
mráz frost
mraznička freezer
mše mass
muzeum museum
muž *n* male
muži men (toilets)
mužský *adj* male
mýdlo soap

N

na for (time)
na zdraví cheers
nábytek furniture
nadobá dish (tableware)
nádor tumor
nádraží train [railway BE] station
nadváha excess luggage
nafta diesel (fuel)
nafukovací matrace air mattress
náhrada *n* refund
náhradní spare (part)
náhradní díl replacement part
náhrdelník necklace
najít find
nakažlivý contagious

nákladní auto truck [lorry BE]
nakojit feed
nákupní košík shopping basket
naléhavý *adj* emergency
nálepka label
náležet belong
náměstí square
napětí voltage
náplast bandage [plaster BE]
napodobenina imitation
naproti opposite
napsat write
náramek bracelet
narodit se born
národní national
narozeniny birthday
nashledanou bye
nástěnka bulletin board
nástupiště platform
náš our(s)
naštěstí fortunately
natržený torn
náušnice earring
navíc spare (extra)
navlhčené ubrousek baby wipe
návod instructions
návštěvní hodiny visiting hours
navštívit *v* visit
nealkoholický non-alcoholic
nebezpečný dangerous
nebo or
něco something
neformální informal (dress)
nehoda accident (road)
nechat si keep
nejbližší next (in a row)

někdy sometimes
nekuřáci non-smoking
nemocnice hospital
nemocný sick [ill BE]
nemrznoucí směs antifreeze
neoprenový oblek wetsuit
nepřetržitý constant
nepříjemný unpleasant
nerv nerve
nervový systém nervous system
nespavost insomnia
nestydatý outrageous
neúmyslně accidentally
neuvěřitelný incredible
nevinný innocent
nezákonné illegal
nezbytný essential
nezdvořilý rude
nic nothing
někdo anyone
nikdy never
nízký low; short (opp. tall)
noc night
noční klub night club
noha leg
nos nose
nosič porter
nouzový východ emergency exit
novinář journalist
novinový stánek newsstand
noviny newspaper
nový new
Nový Zéland New Zealand
nudný boring
nutnost n need
nutný necessary

nůž knife
nůžky scissors
nylon nylon
nyní now

O

obálka envelope
občas occasionally
obdivuhodný amazing
oběd lunch
obchod lihovinami liquor store [off-licence BE]
obchod s obuví shoe store
obchodní centrum shopping mall [centre BE]
obchodní dům department store
obchodní třída business class
objednat order
oblačný cloudy
oblast region (geographical)
oblast s obchody shopping area
oblek suit (man's)
oblíbený favorite
obličej face
obroučky frame (glasses)
obsahovat contain
obsazený full (after meal); occupied
obsluha service (in restaurant)
obtížný hard (difficult)
obyčejný medium (position); regular
obytný přívěs trailer
obývací pokoj living room
od from (time)
odbarvovací prostředek bleach
oddělení ward (hospital)

odečíst deduct (money)
odejít leave (on foot)
odemknout unlock
oděvy clothing store
odjezdová hala departure lounge
odjíždět depart (train, bus)
odlétat depart (plane)
odpadky garbage [rubbish BE]
odpočívat v rest
odstín shade
odšroubovat unscrew
ohlásit report (crime)
ochrnutí paralysis
okenice shutter
okno window
olej oil
olej po opalování after-sun lotion
omlouvat apologize
omyl mistake (misunderstanding)
opálení tan
opalovat se sunbathe
opatrný careful
opera opera
operace operation (medical)
operní divadlo opera house
opravit repair
opravy repairs
optik optician
organizovaný organized
orchestr orchestra
originál genuine
ostrý sharp
ostříhat cut (hair)
osvědčení certificate
ošetřit obličej facial
ošklivý ugly

otec father
oteklina swelling
oteklý swollen
otevírací doba opening hours
otevřený adj open
otrava potravinami food poisoning
otřes mozku concussion
otvírač na láhve bottle opener
otvírač na plechovky can [tin BE]
  opener
otvírat v open
oválný oval
ovoce a zelenina fruit and vegetable
  store [greengrocer BE]

P

pacient n patient
palác palace
palec thumb
palice mallet
palivo fuel
palivové dříví wood
palubní n board
palubní vstupenka boarding card
památková oblast historic site
památník obětem války war memorial
pamětihodnosti sights
pán man
panenka doll
pánev frying pan
paní madam
paní na hlídání děti babysitter
panoráma panorama
pánské plavky swimming trunks
papírnictví stationery store

papírové ubrousky paper napkins
papírový kapesník tissue
papuče slippers
park park
parkovací hodiny parking meter
parkovací služby valet service
parkoviště parking lot [car park BE]
partner partner
pas passport
pásek belt
paže arm
pekařství bakery
pěna na vlasy hair mousse
peníze money
penzión guest house
perla pearl
permanentka na vlek lift pass
pero pen
personál staff
peřej rapids
peřina duvet
pěšák pedestrian
pěší turistika *n* hiking
pěší zóna pedestrian zone [precinct BE]
pěšina footpath
petrolej kerosene
píchlý flat [puncture BE]
piknik picnic
pinzeta tweezers
písek sand
pít *v* drink
pití *n* drink
plán plan
plán metra subway [underground BE] map

pláštěnka raincoat
platba payment
plátek slice
platina platinum
platný valid
plavčík jacket lifeguard
pláž beach
plenka diaper [nappy BE]
plíce lung
plný full (filled)
plomba filling (dental)
plyn butane gas
po after (time); around (place)
pobřeží coast
počasí weather
počet kilometrů není omezen unlimited mileage
počítač computer
počkat wait
pod under
podat na poště *v* post (send)
podívat se see (inspect); visit (see sights)
podlážka groundsheet [groundcloth BE]
podnos tray
podprsenka bra
podrobnosti details
pohlavní nemoc venereal disease
pohlednice postcard
pohodlný comfortable
pojistka insurance card [certificate BE]
pojistná škoda insurance claim
pojištění insurance (car)
pojišťovna insurance (company)

pokoj room
pokojská maid (hotel)
pokožka skin
pokuta fine (penalty)
pole field
poledne noon [midday BE]
políbení *n* kiss
políbit *v* kiss
policejní stanice police station
policie report police
polštář pillow
polyester polyester
pomalý slow
ponožky socks
popálenina *n* burn
popelnice garbage [dustbin BE]
popelník ashtray
popsat describe
populární popular
porce portion
porucha breakdown
porucha trávení indigestion
poschodí floor (level)
poslat *v* mail
poslední *adj* last
postel bed
poškodit damage
pošta *n* mail [post BE]
poštovní poukázka money order
poštovní schránka mailbox
  [postbox BE]
potápěčská maska mask (diving)
potápěčské brýle swimming goggles
potok stream
potom then (time)
potravinová fólie cling film

potraviny grocery store
potřeba *n* need; requirement
potvrdit confirm (reservation);
  validate (tickets)
použít *v* use
povětří *n* air
povlak na polštář pillow case
povlečení sheet (bed)
povolání profession
povolené zboží allowance
pozadu slow (clock)
pozdě late
pozvat invite
požár fire (disaster)
požární hlásič fire alarm
práce job
pračka washing machine
prádelna laundromat
prapodivný bizarre
prarodiče grandparents
prášek na praní washing powder
prášek na spaní sleeping pill
prát *v* **pračce** machine washable
prát *v* **ruce** hand-washable
právník lawyer
pravost authenticity
pravý authentic
prázdný empty
prodávat sell
program program
prohlášení statement (police)
prohlídka sightseeing tour
prohlídka s průvodcem guided tour
projímadlo laxative
projíždět *v* transit
proplatit *v* cash

prosakování *n* leak
prosím please
prosit ask (request)
prostor na přebalování changing facilities
prostředek na mytí nádobí dishwashing liquid
protéza denture
protože because
provize commission
prsa chest (body)
prso breast
prst finger
prst na noze toe
prsten ring
pršet *v* rain
průjem diarrhea
průvodce guide
první třída first class
přátelský friendly
přebalit dítě change (a baby)
před ago
před before (time)
předepsat prescribe
předmět item
přední *adj* front
přednost right of way (in a car)
předpis prescription
předpověď počasí weather forecast
představení *n* play
přehřátí overheat
přechod pro chodce pedestrian crossing
překlad translation
překladatel translator

přeložit translate
přepadení mugging
přes across
přes noc overnight
přestoupit change (transportation)
přibližně approximately
příbory cutlery
přidat join
přihlásit declare
příchuť flavor
příjemný pleasant
přijet arrive (car, train)
přijít call (shout)
příjmení surname
příklad example
přikrývka blanket
přikrývky a povlečení bedding
přiletět arrive (plane)
přímý direct (train, flight)
přirážka supplement
přírodní rezervace nature reserve
přirozenost nature
přistát land (airplane)
přístav harbor
přístupný right of way (access)
příští next (in time)
přitažlivý attractive
přítel friend
příušnice mumps
přívěsek ke klíčům key ring
přivést bring
přízemí first [ground BE] floor
příznak symptom (illness)
pták bird
ptát ask (question)
puchýř blister

půjčit borrow; hire; lend; rent
půjčovna aut car rental
půl half
půlnoc midnight
pumpa pump (gas station)
punčochové kalhoty pantyhose
  [tights BE]
punčochy stockings
pytel na odpadky garbage [rubbish
  BE] bag

R

radnice town hall
raketa racket (tennis, squash)
rakovina cancer (disease)
rameno shoulder
ramínko coat hanger
recepce reception (desk)
recepční receptionist
registrační karta registration form
rekreační středisko holiday resort
rentgen x-ray
repelent proti hmyzu insect repellent
restaurace restaurant
ret lip
revmatismus rheumatism
rezervace reservation
rodiče parents
rodina family
rok year
roleta blind
romantický romantic
rostlina *n* plant
rovný *adj* level
rozbitý broken (damaged)

rozdělovat se share
rozepsaný účet itemized bill
rozmrazit defrost
rozumět understand
rozvedený divorced
rtěnka lipstick
ruční flashlight
ručník towel
ruka hand (body)
rukáv sleeve
rukavice glove
ruksak backpack
růžový pink
rvačka fight (brawl)
rybník pond
rychlý quick
rychlý napřed fast (clock)
řasenka mascara
řeka river
řemesla handicrafts
řetízek chain (necklace)
řezník butcher
řidič driver
řidičský průkaz driver's license

S

s with
s titulky subtitled
sako jacket
sám alone
samoobsluha self-service (gas
  station); supermarket
samostatně separately
sanitka ambulance
satén satin

sauna sauna
sedadlo seat (theater)
sedadlo u okna window seat
sedativum sedative
sedět sit
sejf n safe
sekretářka secretary
sem here (motion)
senná rýma hay fever
servis garage (repair)
sestra sister
sestřenice cousin (female)
setkání appointment
setkat se meet
sever north
sezónní lístek season ticket
schodiště stairs
silnice road
silný strong
silný thick
sjezd exit (highway)
skákat do vody dive
skládací lehátko deck chair
sklenice glass (drinking)
skoro almost
Skotsko Scotland
skupina band (musical group)
skvělý superb
skvrna stain
slabý thin (not thick)
sladký sweet (taste)
slepé střevo appendix
sleva discount
slovník dictionary
sluchadlo hearing aid
slunce sun

sluneční brýle sunglasses
slunečník umbrella (sun)
slušet fit (clothes)
služebná maid (home)
slyšet hear
smaragd emerald
smažený fried
směnárna currency exchange office
směr direction
směrové číslo area code
snad hopefully
snadný easy
sněžit v snow
sníh n snow
snímek exposure (photos)
snubní prstínek wedding ring
socha statue
souhlasit agree
soukromník self-employed
spací pytel sleeping bag
spát sleep
speciál charter flight
specialista specialist
spěšně express
spodní prádlo underwear
Spojené Státy United States
spojení connection (train)
spojit se contact v
spokojený satisfied
společnost company
(companionship); party (social)
spolehlivý reliable
sport sport
sportovní klub sports club
sportovní potřeby sporting goods
store

spravit fix
správný correct
sprcha shower
srdce heart
stadion stadium
stáhnout turn down (volume)
stan tent
stanice stop (bus)
stanice metra subway station
stanové kolíčky tent pegs
stanoviště taxíků taxi stand [rank BE]
staré město old town
starožitnost *n* antique
starší občan senior citizen
starý old
stát se happen
stát *v* cost
statek farm
státní příslušnost nationality
stavět *v* stop
stehno thigh
stejný same
sterilizační roztok sterilizing
  solution
sto hundred
strávit spend (time, money)
strojírenství engineering
strom tree
strýc uncle
střední medium (size)
střecha roof (house, car)
střevo bowel
stříbro silver
student student
studený *adj* cold
studovat study

stůl table
stupeň degree (temperature)
stvrzenka receipt (when paying)
styl style
suit swim
sukně skirt
suterén basement
suvenýr souvenir
sval muscle
svatba wedding
svatebná cestě honeymoon
svědek witness
svědět itch
světlo beam (headlight); light
  (electric)
světlý light (color)
svetr sweater [jumper BE]
svezení lift (hitchhiking)
svléknout se undress
svobodný single (unmarried)
syn son
synagoga synagogue

Š

šachy chess
šálek cup
šampon shampoo
šátek scarf
šatna coatroom
šaty dress
šedý gray
šek *n* check [cheque BE]
široký wide
šnorchl snorkel
šok shock (electric)

špatný bad
špička rush hour
špinavý dirty
šroubovák screwdriver
štěstí luck
štípnutí *n* bite (insect)
štípnutí komárem mosquito bite
šváb cockroach

T

tabák tobacconist
tableta pill
tábořit *v* camp
tady here (place)
také also
talíř plate
tam there
tampon tampon
tančit *v* dance
tanec *n* dance
taxík taxi
téct *v* leak (roof, pipe)
těhotná pregnant
telefon *n* telephone
telefonický hovor telephone call
telefonní budka telephone booth
telefonní číslo telephone number
telefonní karta phone card
telefonní seznam directory (telephone)
telefonovat *v* phone
tělesně postižený *adj* disabled
televize TV
tenis tennis
tenisky sneakers

tenisový kurt tennis court
tenký thin (narrow)
teploměr thermometer
teplota temperature (body)
teplý warm
terasa terrace
termoska thermos flask
těsný tight
teta aunt
tetanus tetanus
těžký difficult; heavy
tichý quiet
tlumočník interpreter
tmavý dark
toaletní papír toilet paper
topení heat
topit se drowning
tradiční traditional
tramvaj tram
trasa line (subway)
tráva grass
tričko sweatshirt
triko T-shirt
trouba oven
tržnice market
tucet dozen
tuhý hard (food)
tunel tunnel
turista tourist
turistická cesta walking route
turistická kancelář tourist office
tvrdý hard (firm)
týden week
tým team
typ *n* type
typický typical

U

u at (place); by (near)
ubrousek napkin
ubytovat se check in (hotel)
ucpaný blocked
účet bill (restaurant)
účet za telefon telephone bill
účetní accountant
učit se learn
učitel teacher
údolí valley
ucho ear
ukázat indicate
ukazatel signpost
ukradený *adj* stolen
ukrást steal
umělý synthetic
umyvadlo sink
unavený tired
uniforma uniform
upravit alter
určitě sure
ústa mouth
úsvit dawn
útes cliff
útok attack
utratit spend (waste)
uvědomit notify
uvnitř inside
uvolnit pokoj check out (hotel)
uzavírací kohout valve
úzký narrow
už already
úžasný great
úžeh sunstroke

užívat take (medicine)

V

v at (time); in (place); on
v důchodu retired
rozbít *v* break
v zahraničí abroad
vadné faulty
vaginální infekce vaginal infection
vagón car (train)
vana *n* bath
vařič stove
vařit *v* cook
včera yesterday
večer evening
večeře dinner
večírek party (event)
vědomí conscious
vedoucí manager
vegetariánský vegetarian
věk age
velikost size
Velké Británie United Kingdom
velkolepý magnificent
velký big
velmi very
velvyslanec ambassador
velvyslanectví embassy
venkovní outdoor
venkovní bazén outdoor pool
venku outside
veřejnost *n* public
vesnice village
vést *v* lead
vestibul lobby (theater, hotel)

větrák fan (ventilation)
vězení prison
věž tower
vhodný suitable
více more
víčko na čočku lens cap
video hra video game
vidět see
vidlička fork
víkend weekend
víkendová sazba weekend rate
vinice vineyard
visací zámek padlock
víta phrase
vítr wind
vitrína display window
vízum visa
vlak train
vlákno na čištění mezizubních prostorů dental floss
vlastnit v own
vlasy hair
vlevo left
vlhkost n damp
vlhký adj damp
vlna wave; wool
voda water
voda po holení aftershave
vodopád waterfall
vodotěsný waterproof
volejbal volleyball
volný available (free); loose
vosa wasp
vozík cart [trolley BE]
vozík na zavazadla luggage cart [trolley BE]

vpředu front (head)
vrátit return (give back)
vrátit peníze v refund
vrátit se return
vrchol peak
vřed ulcer
vřídek n boil (ailment)
vstupné admission charge
vstupní vízum entry visa
všichni all
vtip joke
vybavení equipment (sports); facilities
vybavení na turistiku hiking gear
vybitý dead (battery)
výborný good (delicious)
vyčerpaný exhausted
vyčistit clean v
výdej zavazadel luggage [baggage BE] reclaim
vydržet v last
vyfotografovat photo
vyfoukat blow dry
vyhlídka viewpoint
vycházka s průvodcem guided walk
východ east; exit; gate (airport)
vylekaný afraid
výlet excursion
výlet lodí boat trip
výloha window (store)
vyměnit cash (exchange)
vyplnit fill
vypnout turn off
vyrážka rash
vyslovit pronounce
vysoký high; tall (person)

vystrašený frightened
vyšetření examination (medical)
výška height
vyškolený trained
výtah elevator [lift BE]
vytrhnout (zub) extract (tooth)
vyvolat develop (photos)
vývrtka corkscrew
vyvrtnutý sprained
vyznání religion
vyzvednout collect
vyzvednout si pick up (something)
vyžehlit press
vzadu back (head)
vzbudit wake
vzít take (carry)
vzkaz message
vzorek specimen
vždy always

Z

z from (place)
za after (place); in (within a period of time)
zábava fun
zábavní plavba *n* cruise
zácpa constipation
začátečník beginner
začínat start
začít begin
záda back (body)
zadarmo free (no charge)
zadní rear
zahrada garden
zahraniční měna foreign currency

zahrnovat include
záchod restroom
záchranný člun life boat
záchranný pás life belt
zájem interest (hobby)
zájezd tour
zajímavý interesting
zalogovat log on
záloha deposit
zámek *n* lock
zamknout *v* lock
zamluvit reserve
zánět inflammation
západ west
zápach smell
zápal plíc pneumonia
zapálit *v* smoke
zápalky matches
zapalovač lighter (cigarette)
zápas game; match (sport)
zaplatit pay
zapnout turn on
zapomenout forget
záruka guarantee
zasnoubený engaged
zástrčka plug
zastřihnout trim
zavazadlo luggage [baggage BE]; suitcase
závažný serious
zavírat *v* close
závodní dráha racetrack
zavolat call (telephone)
závrativý dizzy
zavřený *adj* shut
zdravá výživa health food store

zdraví health
zdravotní pojištění health insurance
zdravotní sestra nurse
zdravotní středisko clinic
zem ground (earth)
země country (nation)
zesílit turn up (volume)
zip zipper
zítra tomorrow
zkušební kabina fitting room
zlato gold
zledovatělý icy
zloděj thief
zlomenina fracture
zlomený broken (body part)
změnit *v* change (reservation)
změřit *v* measure
značka sign (road sign)
známka stamp
známý famous
znásilnění rape
znát know
zoo zoo
zopakovat repeat
zpáteční round-trip [return BE]
zpáteční jízdenka round trip [return BE] ticket (train)
zpáteční letenka round trip [return BE] ticket (plane)
zpěvák singer
zpoždění delay
zpráva od policie police report
zrcadlo mirror
zručnost facility
zrušit cancel
zříceniny ruins

ztratit lose
ztráty a nálezy lost-and-found [lost property BE] office
zub tooth
zubař dentist
zubní pasta toothpaste
zůstat stay (remain)
zvětšit enlarge
zvíře animal
zvláštní special
zvlhčující krém moisturizer (cream)
zvracet vomit

Ž

žádný none
žaludeční nevolnost nausea
žaludek stomach
žárovka lightbulb
žebro rib
žebřík ladder
železnice railway
žena *n* female
ženská *adj* female
žíla vein
žít live
život life
žíznivý thirsty
žláza gland

Amanpuri, Thailand

HotelClub.com

JOIN THE CLUB!

Earn Rewards, Get Discounts,
Stay Free, Only with HotelClub!
Across 30,000 Hotels in
120 Countries

£10 OFF
see reverse for details

Berlitz
www.berlitzpublishing.com

Register with

HotelClub.com

and get £10!

At **HotelClub.com**, we reward our Members with discounts and free stays in their favourite hotels. As a Member, every booking made by you through **HotelClub.com** will earn you Member Dollars.

When you register, we will credit your Member Account with **£10* Member Dollars** - which you can use on your next **HotelClub.com** booking. Log on to **www.HotelClub.com/berlitzphrase** to activate your **HotelClub.com** Membership. Complete your details, including the Membership Number & Password located on the back of the **HotelClub.com** card.

Over 4.5 million Members already use Member Dollars to pay for all or part of their hotel bookings. Join now and start spending Member Dollars whenever and wherever you want - you are not restricted to specific hotels or dates!

With great savings of up to 60% on over 30,000 hotels across 120 countries, you are sure to find the perfect location for business or pleasure. Happy travels from **HotelClub.com!**

www.berlitzpublishing.com